WHAT THE BUYER SEES

CLOSING VALUATION GAPS

Joseph P. Lahey

Published by Lahey Growth Capital

Printed in the United States of America

First Edition

ISBN: 9798996897506

Library of Congress Control Number: 2026918028

The cases and examples described in this book are composites drawn from the author's direct operating and advisory experience across multiple companies and sectors. All identifying details have been altered. No account in this book describes any single identifiable individual, company, or transaction.

Cover design by The Book Cover Design

10 9 8 7 6 5 4 3 2 1

This book is dedicated to my wife Diane, who patiently encouraged me to write and complete this book. And to my daughter, Meghan, and my son, Brendan, who listened to my experiences at the dinner table every night.

CONTENTS

Preface 3

Introduction 7

1. The Complexity You Added to Grow Is Now Preventing You From Growing 19
2. Your Financial Statements Are Telling You the Wrong Story 33
3. The Founder's Bandwidth Is the Company's Strategic Ceiling 41
4. Growing Revenue While Shrinking Value 53
5. Most Strategic Plans Are Goal Lists Wearing the Clothes of Strategy 69
6. The Three Initiative Rule 81
7. The Pre Mortem:The Decision Test Your Organization Is Not Running 101
8. Why Your Strategy Looks Different on the Front Line Than It Does in the Boardroom 113
9. How You Sell Changes Everything: The Marketing and Sales Evolution Every Mid-Size Company Must Navigate 131

10. Free Cash Flow: The Number That Determines Everything Else 151

11. The Acquiror's View 173

12. The Margin Leak You Are Funding Without Knowing It 191

13. The Management Team a Buyer Pays For Is Not the One You Think You Have 203

14. The Decision Your Organization Is Avoiding Is the One That Determines Your Outcome 223

15. Your Incentive Structure Is Producing Exactly the Results You Don't Want 243

16. What the Board Sees and What Is Actually Happening Are Usually Different Things 265

17. Private Equity Finds What You Have Not Fixed And Prices It Accordingly 277

18. The Capital Structure That Made Sense at Twenty Million Is Destroying Value at Sixty Million 299

19. Why the Last Two Years Determine the Multiple 309

PREFACE

Books about business are written from many vantage points. Some are written by academics who have studied companies with the rigor of the research institution. Some are written by consultants who have advised companies with the analytical frameworks of the strategy firm. Some are written by journalists who have chronicled companies with the narrative craft of the long form reporter.

This book is written from a different vantage point. It is written from inside the experience of building, running, chairing, financing, and eventually selling mid-sized companies, from inside the specific, daily, sometimes exhilarating and often exhausting reality of being the person responsible for the outcome.

I have been a CEO who sat in the chair when a major market expansion failed in ways that seemed, in retrospect, entirely predictable. I have been a chairman who sat in the boardroom when a strategic plan was approved unanimously and executed poorly. I have been a sponsor who sat on the buying side of the table when a company's capital structure told me more about its owner's financial management sophistication than its investment banker's presentation had intended to reveal. I have been an investor who watched founders leave meaningful value on the table in liquidity events that should have produced better outcomes, not because their businesses were insufficient but because their preparation was.

Two experiences in particular shaped the conviction that runs through this book, and because they illustrate the difference between what a founder believes makes a business valuable and what the people on the other side of the table actually reward, I describe them here.

The Sponsor's Role

I was the sponsor of a 30 million dollar technology company that needed capital to scale. The company had genuinely distinctive technology, and the management team was convinced, reasonably on its face, that the technology was the story the capital markets would buy. When we took the company to investors to raise the growth capital that would let it scale toward 50 million dollars a year, I watched the conversation turn, again and again, away from the technology and toward a single number: free cash flow. The technology was a feature. The free cash flow was the investment. It was not, at the time, improving fast enough, so over the following nine months I worked directly with the management team to change it, not by altering the technology, which was never the issue, but by installing the cash flow disciplines that converted the company's earnings into the cash the investors were underwriting. The improvement over those nine months was substantial, and it was visible in exactly the metric the market cared about. We raised 30 million dollars on the strength of it. The lesson was not subtle, and I have carried it into every engagement since: the founder sells the technology, and the investor buys the free cash flow.

The Chairman's View

I was the board chairman of a publicly traded company, sitting in the chair when the financial management team presented its plan for operating within the Sarbanes Oxley compliance framework. The plan was competent and the team was capable, and the natural inclination of any board is to receive such a plan, approve it, and move on to the next item. But when I probed it, and specifically when we subjected it to the discipline of a pre mortem, asking what this would look like if it had already gone badly wrong, we exposed something the original presentation had not surfaced. The cumulative impact of the compliance program on the company's free cash flow two years down the road was far larger than anyone in the room had ccounted for. The cost was not in the current year, where the board's attention naturally rested. It was in the trailing period that would determine the company's value and its flexibility well after the plan was approved and forgotten. With management's full engagement, we developed a forward looking response: a program to take the company private and delist, executed with shareholder approval, that freed it from a compliance burden whose true cost only the pre mortem had made visible. The lesson was twofold, and I have carried both since. The most important consequences of a decision are often the ones that do not appear in the year you make it. And the question an organization is not asking is usually the one that determines its outcome.

Neither of these was a comfortable conversation in the moment. Both produced outcomes that would not have occurred without the willingness to look past what the business appeared to be and toward what it actually was. That willingness, and the specific disciplines that make it actionable, is the subject of this book.

The lessons in these pages are not derived from research databases or case study archives. They are derived from the experience of being in those rooms, at those tables, in those conversations, making the decisions and watching the consequences, sometimes immediately and sometimes years later. Every insight in these pages was earned. Many of them were earned expensively.

I have shared these lessons over the years in conversations with the founders, CEOs, and senior executives I work with as an operating advisor and principal investor. The quality and consistency of the reception those conversations have received, the recognition that these observations describe something real and important that the standard management literature does not address with the specificity that practitioners require, persuaded me that they warranted a more permanent and more accessible form.

This book is that form. It is written for the executive who does not have time for theory and does not need it, who needs to understand, in specific and actionable terms, the decisions that determine whether a mid-sized company reaches its potential or falls short of it. It is written for the founder navigating the challenges of the growth stage, the CEO building an organization that can execute strategy without depending entirely on personal involvement, the owner approaching a capital event who wants to understand before the process starts what a sophisticated buyer or investor will find, and the financial manager who needs to understand not just what the business earned but what it actually produced.

I have written it in the first person, in the voice of a practitioner rather than an authority, because that is the honest voice for what this material is: the observations of someone who has been there, not the prescriptions of someone who has studied those who were.

INTRODUCTION

There is a stage of a company's development that the management literature has chronically underserved.

It is not the startup stage. The startup ecosystem has generated an enormous body of practical literature, an active practitioner community, and a well-developed support infrastructure of advisors, investors, and educational resources. The founder building a company from zero to ten million dollars in revenue has never had more guidance available.

It is not the large company stage. The management of publicly traded corporations, Fortune 500 companies, and global enterprises is the subject of most of what the business schools teach, most of what the management consultancies publish, and most of what appears in the pages of the major business publications. The executive running a two-billion-dollar company has more frameworks, methodologies, and institutional support than any individual could absorb in a career.

The stage that has been underserved is the one in between: the mid-sized company, typically between 40 million and 300 million dollars in revenue, led by a founder or owner-CEO who built it from the beginning and who now faces a set of management, strategic, and financial challenges that are fundamentally different from the ones he faced at the startup stage, and that the large company literature does not describe with the specificity his situation requires.

This company is large enough to have organizational complexity but not large enough to have the institutional infrastructure that large companies use to manage it. It is sophisticated enough to have competitive strategy but not resourced enough to have a dedicated strategy function to develop and execute it. It is generating enough free cash flow to make real capital allocation choices but not experienced enough to understand what those choices cost in growth foregone or value surrendered. It is successful enough to be approaching a capital event but not experienced enough to understand, without specific preparation, what a sophisticated buyer or investor will find.

The founder or CEO of a mid-sized company is simultaneously the company's chief strategist, primary operational manager, key customer relationship holder, chief talent officer, commercial lead, and as the company approaches a capital event, primary transaction participant. No single role in any of this organizational context combines these demands simultaneously. This book is written for that person.

The mid-sized company executive is not a small version of a large company CEO. He is a fundamentally different kind of executive, operating in a fundamentally different organizational reality, making decisions that the large company literature does not adequately describe and that the startup literature has left behind.

Where These Lessons Come From

My career has given me an unusually complete view of the mid-sized company landscape, because I have encountered it from every significant angle.

I started as a mechanical engineer, which gave me a specific way of looking at organizational and business problems: the habit of decomposing a system into its components and identifying where the failure is occurring, not where management says the failure is occurring. That diagnostic orientation has been the most durable capability I have carried through every subsequent role.

I became a CEO, and then a chairman, of companies that crossed the threshold from mid-sized into significant scale. I experienced firsthand the specific challenges this book describes: the founder's bandwidth ceiling, the organizational complexity that accumulates through growth, the incentive structure that rewards yesterday's behaviors while the strategy requires tomorrow's, the capital structure that was designed for an earlier version of the company and that quietly constrains the current one. I managed free cash flow through periods when the gap between Earnings Before Interest Taxes Depreciation and Amortization ("EBITDA") and actual cash generation was painful and illuminating. I built commercial organizations from the combined selling-delivery-service model of the early stage to the separated, specialized commercial architecture of scale. I did not read about these challenges in a case study. I lived them.

I became a sponsor and private equity participant, which gave me the buyer's view of what sophisticated capital providers see when they evaluate a mid-sized company. I have reviewed hundreds of companies from that side of the table, the capital structure complexity that limited what a genuinely excellent company could raise, the management team assessments that revealed founder dependencies the owner had never formally examined, and the Free Cash Flow ("FCF") conversion rates that told me more about the quality of the business than the EBITDA multiple in the teaser.

I became a principal investor and operating advisor, which gave me the opportunity to work alongside the founders and CEOs navigating these challenges from inside them. This role, more than any of these, has been the laboratory in which the lessons in this book were refined and tested. When you sit with a founder every month for two or three years, helping him navigate the specific decisions that will determine the company's trajectory, you learn what works and what does not with a specificity that no amount of retrospective analysis can produce.

The nineteen articles that form the chapters of this book were each born from this accumulated experience. None of them were written to describe a theory. All of them were written to describe a reality I have encountered directly, in multiple forms, across multiple industries, and at multiple stages of the companies I have worked with.

The Architecture of the Book

The nineteen chapters are organized around five themes that represent the most consequential domains of decision-making for a mid-sized company executive. They are presented in a sequence that builds from the most immediate and operational to the most strategic and financial, because that is the order in which their consequences typically become visible. But they are simultaneous, interdependent, and mutually reinforcing in practice.

Theme One: The Operational Reality That Growth Creates

The first four chapters address the specific operational challenges that accumulate as a company grows — the stage at which the management practices that produced the growth become the constraints on the next phase.

The Complexity You Added to Grow Is Now Preventing You From Growing

How the decisions that produced a company's growth accumulate into complexity that stalls the next phase. The four complexity patterns, the 80/20 diagnostic, and the four practices that eliminate complexity before it eliminates momentum are reviewed.

Your Financial Statements Are Telling You the Wrong Story

The management reliance on lagging financial statements and its specific costs. The five leading operational signals that predict financial performance weeks before the P&L shows it. The six practices that build a forward-looking management information system are discussed.

The Founder's Bandwidth Is the Company's Strategic Ceiling

How the founder's finite management capacity becomes the binding constraint on strategic growth. The bandwidth calculation, the three phases of founder-led growth, and the subtract-before-add framework are presented.

Growing Revenue While Shrinking Value: The ROIC Problem Most CEOs Ignore

How a company can grow revenue consistently while destroying enterprise value. The ROIC and value spread calculations, the three operational drivers, and the five practices for incorporating capital efficiency into growth strategy are reviewed.

Theme Two: Strategy That Gets Executed

The next four chapters address the specific failures of the strategic planning and execution process in mid-sized companies — from the planning document that produces no organizational change to the front-line employee who cannot describe how his daily decisions connect to the company's strategic direction.

Most Strategic Plans Are Goal Lists Wearing the Clothes of Strategy

Why mid-sized company strategic plans consistently fail to produce organizational change. The diagnosis-first framework, the three questions a useful strategic plan must answer, and the one-page strategy format are discussed.

The Three-Initiative Rule: Why Doing Less Produces More

How post-success overcommitment produces stalled organizations. The mathematics of initiative overcommitment, the four symptoms of initiative overload, and the six disciplines that restore strategic focus are explored.

The Pre-Mortem: The Decision Test Your Organization Is Not Running

Gary Klein's prospective hindsight methodology applied to mid-sized company decisions is presented. The five decision categories that require a pre-mortem, the six-step protocol, and the governance requirement that makes the practice institutional are defined.

Why Your Strategy Looks Different on the Front Line Than It Does in the Boardroom

The communication-versus-translation distinction. The five gaps through which strategic intent loses meaning between the boardroom and the front line, and the six practices that make strategy executable at every level are defined.

Theme Three: The Commercial Engine

The next two chapters address the marketing and sales disciplines that are most consistently underinvested and most consequentially mismanaged in mid-sized companies and the ability to convert sales into Free Cash. The go-to-market architecture that determines whether the company's commercial performance is built for its current scale or for the one it left behind.

How You Sell Changes Everything: The Marketing and Sales Evolution Every mid-sized Company Must Navigate

The fundamental differences between selling services, products, and technology, i.e. different people, different cycles, different owner roles are analyzed. The four commercial evolution stages from combined selling-delivery-service to mature separated functions are examined. Marketing's evolution from referral economy to institutional demand generation are analyzed. The owner's commercial role across the scaling journey are defind.

Free Cash Flow: The Number That Determines Everything Else

Why EBITDA and free cash flow diverge and what drives the gap. Daily and weekly cash management including receivables discipline, payables trade-offs, and the thirteen-week forecast as an operational instrument are suggested. FCF as the foundation of debt renewal and credit quality and how FCF's role changes as the business scales plus its central function in transaction valuation and liquidity event structure are examined.

Theme Four: Value Creation and Transaction Preparation

The next five chapters address the specific value creation disciplines that determine what a mid-sized company is worth and the specific preparation practices that ensure that value is recognized and realized in a capital event.

The Acquiror's View: What Sophisticated Buyers See in Your Business That You Don't

The five elements that a sophisticated acquiror examines: normalized EBITDA, management depth, revenue quality, competitive moat, and financial reporting quality. Why three to five years of preparation is not cautious but necessary.

The Margin Leak You Are Funding Without Knowing It

The five sources of the gap between reported and normalized EBITDA in mid-sized private companies. The compounding mathematics of the margin leak and the five-step self-diagnostic protocol.

The Management Team a Buyer Pays For Is Not the One You Think You Have

The builder-versus-scaler distinction is presented. The six-question management transferability assessment, the failure modes of outside talent integration, and the five practices that build genuine management depth are defined.

The Decision Your Organization Is Avoiding Is the One That Determines Your Outcome

The pattern of decision avoidance in mid-sized organizations is delineted. Five avoidance categories, the political economy of deferral, and the five practices that create an organization that decides are examined.

Your Incentive Structure Is Producing Exactly the Results You Don't Want

How the natural drift between compensation plan design and current strategic priorities produces behaviors that undermine the strategy being executed. The alignment audit and the political disciplines of compensation redesign are presented.

Theme Five: The Disciplines of the Diagnostic Practitioner

The final four chapters address the specific diagnostic, governance, and leadership disciplines that distinguish the executives who consistently make better decisions from those who manage the consequences of inadequate ones.

What the Board Sees and What Is Actually Happening Are Usually Different Things

The systematic information asymmetries of mid-sized private company board governance from both the chairman's and the executive's perspective is discussed. Five information gaps and six practices that close them are defined.

Private Equity Finds What You Have Not Fixed — And Prices It Accordingly

What PE diligence finds in mid-sized company transactions and what each finding costs. The deal structure consequences of deferred problems and the seller's self-diligence framework are contrasted.

The Capital Structure That Made Sense at $20 Million Is Destroying Value at $60 Million

How financing decisions made at an earlier stage become structural constraints. The four most damaging capital structure mismatches, the growth capital provider's perspective, and the refinancing sequence.

The Two Years Before the Exit Are Worth More Than the Twenty Before Them

The trailing period asymmetry in transaction valuation is reviewed. The operating-versus-asset-building mindset shift and the eight-quarter preparation roadmap and the personal transformation the two-year window requires are defined.

There are abbreviations used throughout the book: Chief Executive Officer ("CEO"), Chief Operating Officer ("COO") and Human Resources ("HR"). Other abbreviations are included in respective texts.

The Thread That Runs Through All of It

Reading these nineteen chapters as a collection rather than as independent articles, a thread becomes visible that I want to name explicitly, because it is the most important thing this book is ultimately about.

Every chapter is, at its core, about the gap between what a company appears to be and what it actually is. The gap between the strategic plan and the organizational behavior it produces. The gap between the financial statements and the operational reality that generated them. The gap between EBITDA and free cash flow, between what the business earned and what it actually produced in cash. The gap between the commercial model that served the company at twenty million dollars and the one it needs at sixty million. The gap between the management team the founder believes he has and the management team a sophisticated buyer assesses. The gap between the capital structure that appears manageable and the strategic constraints it imposes. The gap between the business presented in the investment banker's document and the business that diligence reveals.

These gaps are not the product of dishonesty. They are the product of the natural human tendency to see our own businesses through the lens of our investment in them, to see what we hoped to build rather than precisely what exists. This tendency is not a flaw. It is the same optimism and conviction that makes founders build companies in the first place. It is, however, a tendency that has a specific cost when it prevents the honest diagnostic assessment that every consequential management decision requires.

The discipline that runs through every chapter of this book is the discipline of honest diagnosis. Not the comfortable diagnosis, not the politically acceptable diagnosis, not the diagnosis that validates existing management assumptions, but the honest one. The one that requires the same willingness to examine an organization's actual condition that an engineer brings to a system failure, that a physician brings to a clinical presentation, that a sophisticated investor brings to a due diligence process.

I have found, in every domain this book addresses, that the gap between a company's actual condition and its potential is almost always findable. The margin leak is in the financial statements if you look for it honestly. The FCF conversion problem is in the working capital cycle if you calculate it specifically. The founder dependency is visible in the transferability assessment if you apply it rigorously. The commercial model mismatch is identifiable in the sales cycle data if you examine it against the right benchmarks. The capital structure mismatch is calculable if you ask the right five questions.

The findings are available. What varies is the willingness to look.

Every gap described in this book is findable, and most are fixable. The ones that cannot be fixed can be managed if they are found early enough. The ones that are found too late become the price adjustments, the deal structure complications, the earnout disputes, and the valuation disappointments that represent the most expensive tuition available in business.

How to Read This Book

Each chapter stands alone. A CEO wrestling with initiative overcommitment can read Chapter Six without reading the prior five. A founder preparing for a capital event in eighteen months can read

Chapters Eleven through Fifteen as a preparation curriculum. A CFO wanting to understand free cash flow management in the context of growth, debt, and transaction value can read Chapter Ten as a standalone financial management guide.

At the same time, the chapters are deliberately integrated. The complexity that accumulates in Chapter One creates the bandwidth constraint that Chapter Three describes. The commercial architecture that Chapter Nine describes determines the customer concentration risk that Chapter Twelve must address before a transaction. The free cash flow that Chapter Ten defines is the foundation of the debt renewal conversation that Chapter Fifteen's capital structure analysis depends on. The management depth that Chapter Thirteen builds is what the PE diligence in Chapter Fourteen will assess. The two-year preparation window in Chapter Nineteen consolidates the work described in Chapters Eleven through Fifteen into a single operational framework.

Reading the book as a whole produces a picture of the mid-sized company's full challenge landscape that reading any individual chapter does not. The picture it produces is neither hopeless nor reassuring. It is honest. And honest, in my experience, is always the most useful place to start.

A Note on Voice and Form

This book is written in the first person because the experiences it describes were first-person experiences. I was in the room when the strategic plan failed. I was at the table when the capital structure complexity prevented the growth capital raise. I was on the buying side when the diligence process found what the investment banker's presentation had not addressed. I managed free cash flow through periods when the number told an uncomfortable story about a business I had thought was performing well. I built commercial organizations from the combined early-stage model to the separated architecture of scale, and made the hiring mistakes that the article on selling services, products, and technology was written to prevent.

The cases and examples throughout the book are composites. Every situation reflects a real pattern observed across multiple companies, industries, and development stages. The details have been altered to protect the individuals and organizations involved, and the specific financial figures are illustrative of the range rather than exact records of any single situation. But none of the patterns are invented. All of them were observed.

The voice throughout is the voice of a practitioner speaking to practitioners directly, without qualification, in the specific terms that management decisions actually require. I have resisted the academic's instinct to hedge every observation with a literature review and the consultant's instinct to systematize every insight into a proprietary framework. What I have tried to produce is the book I would have wanted to read twenty years ago, when the experiences that generated its lessons were still ahead of me.

It would have saved me considerable expense. I offer it in the hope that it will do the same for you.

1

THE COMPLEXITY YOU ADDED TO GROW IS NOW PREVENTING YOU FROM GROWING

WHAT GOT YOU HERE CAN HOLD YOU BACK.

The phone call came on a Tuesday afternoon from a founder I had known for several years. His company had grown from $eight million to $42 million in revenue in six years. He had built a genuinely impressive regional services business with a loyal customer base, a capable team, and margins that had once ranked among the best in its sector.

He called because growth had stalled for the second year in a row and he could not explain why. The market was still healthy. Customers were still spending. The team was still working hard. Yet every growth initiative seemed to bog down somewhere in the middle of the organization. New products moved too slowly, launched too late, and underdelivered. New market efforts absorbed time and capital and produced little. Important sales opportunities were lost to competitors that simply moved faster. In his words, he felt like he was pushing on a rope.

Before offering a diagnosis, I asked him one question: how many products does your company sell today compared with three years ago? He paused. Three years earlier, the answer had been eleven. Now it was twenty seven. He had noticed each addition as it happened, and each had seemed reasonable on its own. What he had not noticed was the cumulative effect.

That is how complexity enters a growing company. It does not arrive dramatically. It shows up as a long series of rational decisions that make sense one at a time and become destructive in aggregate. Over time, those decisions quietly turn the organization that enabled growth into the organization that now resists it.

I have seen this pattern throughout my career, running companies, chairing boards, and advising founders of mid-sized businesses trying to grow beyond the point where growth becomes structurally difficult. The complexity trap is not usually the fate of weak companies. It is more often the inheritance of successful ones. The businesses most vulnerable to it are the ones that grew fastest, added most aggressively, and never developed the discipline to subtract.

Complexity arrives quietly, one reasonable decision at a time, until the organization becomes the obstacle.

The Frustration Nobody Names

Every founder of a mid-sized company eventually has the same experience, even if they never describe it this way.

You are in a management meeting reviewing a strategic initiative launched six months earlier. It is behind schedule. The team responsible for it can explain why in detail: competing priorities, limited resources, a market development that required a shift in approach, coordination problems with another function. Every explanation is plausible. Most of them are partly true. The initiative is still behind schedule.

You leave the meeting with a feeling that is hard to name. It is not quite anger. It is not exactly disappointment with any one person. It is closer to the sensation of leaning against something that gives just enough to suggest progress but never truly moves. Effort goes in. Momentum never comes out.

That is the lived experience of organizational complexity. It is what it feels like to run a company with more moving parts than any one leader or initiative can navigate cleanly. In my experience, it is one of the most demoralizing moments in the life of a business, not because the company is collapsing, but because it is slowing in a way that is difficult to diagnose and even harder to fix directly.

The hardest truth for founders to accept is that the resistance is usually not personal. The people slowing down growth initiatives are rarely anti growth. They are trying to manage the legitimate demands of an operating environment that the company itself created. Their jobs have multiplied, fragmented, and become so interconnected that doing them responsibly often conflicts with the speed and coordination the next phase of growth requires.

That distinction matters. A performance problem calls for talent changes. An architecture problem calls for structural intervention. In most mid-sized companies wrestling with complexity, the issue is architectural. Yet founders often reach first for personnel changes because they are more familiar and feel more actionable.

New hires are brought in. Consultants are engaged. Training programs are launched. Performance systems are tightened. These interventions often help briefly because they add energy and attention to a system whose underlying architecture is unchanged. When that burst of energy fades, the slowness returns. The founder becomes more frustrated, and the organization becomes less confident that leadership truly understands the source of the drag.

The people slowing you down aren't resisting growth. They're trying to work responsibly inside a structure your growth created.

How Complexity Accumulates

The complexity that stalls growth is not random. It tends to build through four recurring patterns. Each comes from the same instinct that produced the company's success in the first place: a bias toward adding and a reluctance to remove anything that once appeared useful.

What matters is not simply seeing these patterns, but recognizing when they have moved past the point of productive management and started to tax the company's ability to execute.

Complexity Type 1 Product and Service Proliferation

What it looks like: A portfolio that was once compact becomes crowded. The company keeps adding products or services because customers ask for them, competitors offer them, or sales believes a new variation will open another segment. Very few offerings are ever formally retired. Before long, a large portion of the line generates little revenue while consuming a disproportionate share of operations, support, and management attention.

What it costs: Every additional offering creates fixed overhead across the organization: planning, quality control, customer support, billing, training, and sales knowledge. The real cost is not the direct cost of the item itself. It is the attention every function must keep spending to support it. That attention is no longer available for the initiatives most likely to drive growth.

Complexity Type 2 Customer Portfolio Fragmentation

What it looks like: A company that once served a small number of attractive customer segments gradually starts saying yes to almost everyone willing to buy. Sales celebrates each new logo. Operations and service quietly absorb the demands of accounts whose economics do not justify the effort required to support them. The result is a customer base that is broader than it is healthy.

What it costs: Fragmented portfolios create friction in every customer facing function. Sales has to manage too many account types with too many value propositions. Service teams spread themselves thin across incompatible needs. Management loses the ability to distinguish profitable customers from unprofitable ones and therefore loses the ability to allocate effort intelligently.

Complexity Type 3 Process Proliferation

What it looks like: A decision that once required one signature now needs four. Pricing that used to sit with a sales leader now goes to a committee. A hire that once took a week now takes six. Each extra step was added for a reason, often after a pricing miss, a bad hire, or a budget problem. In isolation, each control makes sense. In aggregate, they produce an organization that moves far more slowly than the market around it.

What it costs: Process complexity is especially dangerous because every step has a defensible origin story. What no one calculates is the total drag those controls create together. The business starts responding to opportunities in weeks instead of days, and through committees instead of judgment. Fast competitors are not always smarter. They are often simply carrying less approval architecture.

Complexity Type 4 Organizational Layer Accumulation

What it looks like: As headcount grows, management layers multiply. Each layer is added to solve a span of control problem. Each new manager naturally adds meetings, updates, and coordination work that help justify the layer's existence. Information that once moved from the front line to the CEO in one conversation now passes through multiple filters before it reaches someone able to act.

What it costs: Layers slow organizations not through bad intent but through normal managerial behavior: the need to stay informed, stay involved, and add value. Each layer becomes a tollbooth in communication and decision making. By the time a customer signal or competitive opportunity has passed through enough layers, it often arrives softened, delayed, and stripped of the urgency that should have driven action.

The Organization Does Not Know It Is Slowing Growth

This is the part of the diagnosis that founders find hardest to accept and that matters most: the people creating friction around growth initiatives are usually not doing so intentionally. They are not resisting growth. They are not defending turf. They are responding rationally to the environment they work in.

The product manager who takes six months to launch something new is not necessarily lacking urgency. He may be juggling 14 active projects, each with a legitimate internal sponsor, inside an approval process that requires time from functions whose calendars are just as overloaded as his. The sales manager who loses an opportunity because pricing took three weeks to approve is not indifferent to winning. He is operating inside a control structure built to prevent the margin mistakes of three years ago, a structure no one has reexamined against the competitive cost of delay.

This is the defining feature of complexity as a growth inhibitor: it turns individually rational behavior into collectively irrational outcomes. People make reasonable decisions within the environment they have. The environment itself is what has become counterproductive. And that environment was built by the same growth decisions that made the company successful.

When I work with a leadership team trying to diagnose a growth stall, the most revealing question is not what is going wrong. It is what is unexpectedly going right. I ask each executive to describe the last time something moved faster than expected. The answers usually cluster around the same exceptions: a senior leader bypassed the normal process, a customer emergency created temporary permission to move, or a small team operated outside the usual coordination structure long enough to get something done.

Those moments matter because they prove the people are capable of speed. The architecture is not. The constraint is structural, not human.

The constraint isn't your people. It's the architecture — which is harder to fix, and easier to ignore.

The 80/20 Diagnosis

The first step in reducing complexity is making it visible. That sounds obvious, but most organizations never see complexity in aggregate because it was introduced incrementally. No one keeps a running count of how many products are still actively supported, how many approvals a routine decision now requires, or how many layers a customer signal passes through before it reaches the person who can act on it. The data exists. It is rarely assembled in a way that supports structural decisions.

The most useful diagnostic tool I have found is a simple 80/20 analysis applied to the product portfolio, the customer base, and the company's process architecture. The results are remarkably consistent. Roughly 20 percent of the products, customers, and process variations generate the overwhelming share of the revenue, margin, and productive energy. The remaining portion consumes a disproportionate amount of operational attention while contributing only modest financial value.

Management teams are often surprised by how clear the pattern becomes once it is laid out. The initial reaction is usually discomfort, because the analysis implies that a meaningful share of what the company does every day is not worth continuing. That discomfort is productive. It is the starting point for the structural intervention that talent upgrades, process improvement campaigns, and change programs rarely deliver.

The 80/20 analysis is not a formula that automatically tells you what to eliminate. It is a disciplined way to force the team to look at its portfolio of activities with the same seriousness it brings to capital allocation. In companies that do this work well, the list of things that should stop is almost always longer than anyone expected.

The 80 20 Question	What the Answer Reveals
Which 20 percent of our products generate 80 percent of our gross margin?	The lines the company should protect, invest in, and scale, along with the lower value offerings whose removal would free capacity without materially weakening performance.
Which 20 percent of our customers generate 80 percent of our profitable revenue?	The customer profile worth replicating and the accounts consuming service resources at economics no one has formally challenged.
Which 20 percent of our process steps account for 80 percent of our decision delays?	The approvals and coordination routines whose removal would most improve speed without reintroducing the risks they were designed to control.
Which 20 percent of our management meetings generate 80 percent of the decisions that actually change how the company operates?	The cadence worth preserving and the meetings that absorb time while producing little more than status reporting.

Four Practices That Eliminate Complexity Before It Eliminates Growth

The solutions are not conceptually difficult. What makes them hard is psychological. They require founders and management teams to let go of products they launched, customers they once celebrated, controls they fought to install, and layers they built to manage growing headcount. For leaders who built their companies by adding, the discipline of subtraction feels unnatural. Yet subtraction is exactly what restores organizational capacity. Applied consistently, the following practices address the most common forms of growth killing complexity and help keep them from returning.

Solution 1 Annual Portfolio Rationalization

The action: Once each year, leadership should review every product, service, and customer segment using the 80/20 lens. Offerings that fall in the bottom tier on gross margin contribution and strategic relevance should be evaluated for retirement, consolidation, or explicit conditional retention. Bottom tier customer accounts should be evaluated using a fully loaded cost to serve view. Where service burden exceeds contribution, the company should reprice, restructure, or transition the relationship.

The outcome: The first rationalization often frees 15 to 25 percent of operational capacity that had been trapped in the bottom layer of the portfolio. The cost savings matter, but the bigger gain is the organizational energy released for higher value growth work.

Solution 2 The Process Speed Audit

The action: Map each routine decision that takes more than five business days from start to finish. Document the current approval path, the original reason each step was added, and how often in the past year that step actually prevented the problem it was designed to stop. Then compare that with how often the process delayed a meaningful opportunity. Steps whose prevention record does not justify their delay cost should be removed, delegated downward, or replaced with a post decision audit outside standard parameters.

The outcome: Companies that run this audit often discover that 40 to 60 percent of their approval steps are guarding against risks that have not materialized in years while adding predictable delay to every decision in the category. Streamlining those steps can cut decision time dramatically without increasing error in a meaningful way.

Solution 3 The Management Layer Review

The action: Draw the real organizational chart, not the formal one on paper but the one that reflects how decisions are actually made and how information actually flows. Count the layers between the CEO and the front line. Then ask, for each layer, what decisions it makes that cannot be made below it and what information it adds that would otherwise be lost. If a layer cannot answer those questions clearly, it is functioning mainly as coordination infrastructure. As complexity falls, the need for that layer should be reconsidered.

The outcome: This review is politically sensitive because it touches people rather than products or processes. It should therefore be framed as an architecture exercise, not a performance exercise. The goal is not necessarily lower headcount. It is a wider span of decision authority closer to customers and markets.

Solution 4 The Addition Rule

The action: Before any new product, customer segment, process step, or management layer is added, the team should identify what will be removed, consolidated, or simplified to make room for it. The rule does not block growth. It blocks the kind of growth that creates complexity without creating enough value to justify the attention it consumes.

The outcome: This rule changes the conversation from Should we add this to What will we stop doing so we can support this well. That second question is one of the most revealing strategic disciplines a management team can adopt because it forces explicit tradeoffs instead of silent accumulation.

What Subtraction Actually Produces

Most management teams hesitate because they fear subtraction will make the company smaller rather than stronger. The concern is understandable. Every product retired represents a prior investment. Every low value customer that is restructured was once booked as a win. Every approval step removed was originally added to solve a real problem. On an individual level, subtraction feels like loss.

The real question is whether those losses are smaller or larger than the capacity they release. In company after company, I have seen the same answer. The products removed in a first rationalization often represent a modest share of revenue and an even smaller share of gross margin, while consuming an outsized share of operational attention across sales, service, finance, and management. Once removed, the company regains capacity that can be redirected toward the lines that actually matter.

The same pattern appears in customer portfolios. The bottom tier of accounts usually contributes modest revenue and substantial service complexity. Tightening the portfolio often leads to a short term revenue dip that is offset within a year through better retention and deeper expansion among the customers most worth serving.

Process simplification tends to produce the fastest visible results because it addresses the founder's daily experience most directly. When the approval architecture is stripped back, initiatives that used to stall in the middle of the organization begin to move at the pace the market requires. The rope stops resisting and starts pulling.

Every product retired, every low value customer restructured, and every unnecessary approval step removed is organizational capacity released back to the growth agenda

The Governing Principle

The founder of the $42 million services company I mentioned earlier eventually cut his active product count from twenty seven to fourteen over the next eighteen months. He rationalized the customer portfolio, removing sixty three accounts that produced negative margin on a fully loaded basis. He took four approval steps out of the new product process and two out of pricing. He flattened the management structure from six layers to four.

Revenue fell four percent in the first year and grew 19 percent in the second. Gross margin expanded by six points. The time from strategic decision to operational launch fell by 40 percent. Two years later, he told me the company felt the way it had at $22 million in revenue: fast, focused, and capable of acting on the opportunities in front of it.

That is the most accurate description I know of what subtracting complexity actually delivers. It does not make the business feel smaller. It makes it feel focused. And focus is what allows a company to grow into something genuinely larger.

I have come to think of complexity management as the discipline that makes every other management discipline possible. A company that is too complex cannot execute strategy because management bandwidth is consumed by coordination. It cannot develop leaders because managers spend their time navigating complexity rather than coaching teams. It cannot respond quickly to competitors because its decision structure was built for caution rather than speed.

Remove enough complexity and those other disciplines become available again. The strategy can be executed because the organization has room to execute it. Managers can develop because the system is simple enough to master. Opportunities can be seized because the approval path is lean enough to permit real action.

Every founder I have seen work through this process describes the same emotion at the end: not regret over what was removed, but relief.

Relief that the company once again moves at the pace the opportunity requires. Relief that growth initiatives are met with response rather than friction. Relief that the rope has started to pull.

> ***Growth requires addition. Sustained growth requires subtraction.***

Summary

Complexity is the accumulated cost of every decision that added capability at one stage of a company's development without being tested for its fit at the next. It rarely announces itself as a crisis. It shows up instead as a slower organization, a wider cost base, and a management team that spends more time coordinating than creating.

The companies that move through this stage do not do so by managing complexity more elegantly. They do so by identifying the structures, activities, and decisions that have stopped earning their organizational cost and removing them with the same deliberateness that once added them. Revenue and margin record the consequences of those choices.

But the company's actual ability to move in real time, how quickly it decides, how clearly it sees, and how much management attention is still available for growth rather than maintenance, depends on something even more immediate than the numbers themselves. The next chapter examines that question directly through the lens of whether the financial information the company relies on is telling the right story at all.

2

Your Financial Statements Are Telling You the Wrong Story

Being right about yesterday won't prepare you for tomorrow.

The monthly P&L, the quarterly balance sheet, and the annual audit are excellent at one thing: documenting decisions you already made. But most CEOs do not fail because they misunderstood the past. They fail because they reacted too late to what was changing in the business while the numbers still looked fine.

One of my longest running frustrations in business is how often capable management teams try to run companies with information built for a different purpose. Financial statements are essential. They are standardized, disciplined, and trustworthy. But they are not designed to help a CEO see what is developing inside the business in time to act on it.

That distinction matters more than most leaders admit. By the time a monthly financial package reaches the chief executive, the events it describes are often several weeks old. The operational conditions that produced those results began forming even earlier. In other words, the company is often using an accurate record of yesterday to make decisions about tomorrow.

This is not a theoretical problem. It is one of the main reasons mid-sized companies drift into margin pressure, customer attrition, cash strain, and talent loss before leadership recognizes what is happening. The evidence was usually there. It just was not sitting in the monthly close package.

Financial statements are excellent reporting tools. They are poor early warning systems.

The real flaw is not accuracy. It is timing.

Most executives do not overestimate the accuracy of financial statements. They overestimate their usefulness as management instruments. The P&L tells you what happened. It does not tell you which customer relationships are quietly weakening, which discounting habits are spreading in the sales force, or which operating bottlenecks are starting to erode service quality.

Revenue is reported as a total. Gross margin appears as a blended percentage. Cost of goods sold is a line item. That level of aggregation is appropriate for reporting, but not for proactive decision making. A CEO rarely needs only a clean historical summary. A CEO needs to know where the pressure is building and how much time is left to respond.

This is why so many management conversations start too late. When the main artifact in the room is the monthly P&L, the conversation naturally begins with the same question: What happened? That is a useful question for accountability. It is the wrong starting point for managing a fast moving business.

What lagging information costs

Pricing

Margin compression rarely begins in the month it first appears in the P&L. It usually starts much earlier through small changes in discounting behavior, customer mix, supplier pricing, or production efficiency. By the time the blended margin number falls enough to trigger concern, the habits and expectations behind it are already embedded.

The damage is not just financial. It is managerial. A pricing correction that would have been straightforward at the first signal becomes harder after several months of commercial drift.

Talent

The same pattern appears in talent. The financial consequences of employee attrition such as recruiting costs, lower productivity, and weaker customer service come well after the actual risk became visible. People often signal disengagement before they resign. Participation declines. Development conversations slow. Discretionary effort fades. None of that shows up in the income statement.

A management team that watches those signals has a window to act. A team that waits for the financial consequences does not.

Customers

Customer loss is perhaps the clearest example. A major account does not disappear the moment the final invoice is processed. The relationship usually deteriorates first through lower order frequency, slower buyer responsiveness, more service complaints, or sharper pricing pressure. The business sees the symptoms long before finance records the revenue loss.

That is why the most expensive decisions in a mid-sized company are often the ones made after the evidence becomes visible in the financial statements. At that point, leadership is not steering the business. It is absorbing the consequences.

The most expensive management mistakes are often made after the operating evidence was already available.

Five signals that deserve a seat beside the P&L

Sales velocity and pipeline quality. Current revenue reflects deals that closed weeks or months ago. Pipeline velocity, stage movement, and conversion quality give management a much earlier read on the next quarter. A pipeline can look healthy in total value while quietly weakening in speed and probability. CEOs need both measures.

Customer purchase frequency and volume trends. A flat revenue line can conceal early deterioration inside the installed base. Tracking order cadence and volume by account reveals which customers are healthy, which are softening, and which have begun to disengage before the decline shows up in aggregate revenue.

Margin by transaction, customer, and product. Blended gross margin is a lagging summary. Transaction level margin is a management tool. It exposes where discounting is expanding, which products are underperforming, and which customer segments are dragging profitability before the problem spreads through the full book.

Operational throughput and delivery performance. On time delivery, cycle time, defect rates, rework, and backlog aging are not just operating metrics. They are advance indicators of future customer satisfaction, future service cost, and future retention. When these metrics slip, the financial consequences usually follow.

Working capital velocity. The balance sheet shows position at month end. It does not show momentum. Receivables aging and days sales outstanding trends provide a much earlier view of whether the business is drifting toward a cash problem. That lead time is often the difference between controlled intervention and emergency financing.

How to build a forward looking management system

The answer is not to replace financial statements. Companies need them for governance, tax, lender communication, investor confidence, and basic discipline. The answer is to stop pretending they are enough.

What most mid-sized companies need is a parallel management system that is simpler, faster, and rooted in operating reality. In practice, that system usually begins with a weekly operating review built around a fixed set of leading signals. It is short, structured, and repetitive by design. The point is not to produce more analysis. The point is to create a rhythm in which emerging issues are visible early and discussed before they harden into results.

That review works best when it is paired with a single page signal report. Most management packets are too long, too dense, and too backward looking. A useful weekly report should be easy to scan in minutes. It should tell leadership what is moving, which direction it is moving, and where intervention is needed.

Companies should also shorten the monthly close wherever possible. A ten day close does not solve the timing problem, but it does reclaim valuable decision time. The gain is practical, not cosmetic. When a business moves from a twenty day close to a ten day close, leadership gets earlier visibility into issues that might still be correctable.

Finally, every mid-sized company should maintain a rolling 13 week cash flow forecast and a rolling four quarter operating forecast. Annual budgets are still useful as planning tools, but they are weak instruments for managing a changing business. Rolling forecasts force management to confront current conditions rather than defend outdated assumptions.

What changes when the conversation changes

The real payoff is not simply faster information. It is a different kind of management conversation. When leaders rely primarily on lagging financial reports, they spend most of their time explaining variance and diagnosing outcomes that are already fixed in the past. When they review leading operating signals, they spend more of their time asking what is developing and what action is still available.

That shift is subtle at first, but profound over time. Management attention moves toward problems while they are still correctable and opportunities while they are still actionable. The company becomes less reactive, not because its leaders are smarter, but because they are finally looking at information that lets them act before the fact instead of after it.

In my experience, teams that make this shift do not suddenly become perfect. They still miss forecasts, lose customers, and make bad calls. But they do those things less often, and when trouble emerges they see it sooner. In operating terms, that is often the difference between a manageable problem and a quarter defining one.

A practical dashboard for forward looking management

The table below shows the core metrics that belong in a weekly management rhythm. None requires new software. Each can be assembled from systems most companies already have.

Review cadence	Signal	What it helps predict
Weekly	Pipeline velocity and stage movement	Revenue performance over the next 8 to 12 weeks
Weekly or every other week	Account purchase frequency and volume	Customer retention risk before it appears in reported revenue
Weekly	Transaction level margin	Blended margin deterioration before it reaches the monthly P&L
Weekly	On time delivery, cycle time, and rework	Service quality, cost pressure, and renewal risk
Weekly	Receivables aging and DSO trend	Cash flow pressure 60 to 90 days ahead
Monthly	Customer health score	Renewal and churn risk across the installed base
Weekly	Rolling 13 week cash forecast	Near term liquidity and timing of cash constraints
Monthly	Rolling four quarter forecast	Forward revenue and profit trajectory based on current assumptions
Monthly	Monthly P&L	Historical performance, governance, and accountability

Summary

Financial statements are not the enemy. They remain essential. But they are telling leaders a story about what has already happened, and too many management teams stop there.

The better question is not whether the numbers are accurate. It is whether the company is also paying attention to the operating signals that reveal what is about to happen next. In most businesses, those signals already exist. The real choice is whether leadership will elevate them into the management system.

That choice does not require a new platform, a large consulting project, or a major capital commitment. It requires a different discipline. For CEOs who want earlier warning, better timing, and more useful management conversations, that discipline is one of the highest return changes they can make.

The financial statements of a company are a record of what happened. They are optimized for accuracy, reporting discipline, and tax compliance, and they are delivered on a timetable that makes them useful for governance and completely insufficient for day to day operating decisions.

A CEO who navigates primarily by quarterly financials is navigating with a map of where the company was 60 to 90 days ago. The problem is not the statements themselves. They do their job well. The problem is relying on them as the primary management instrument when the leading signals that predict where the business is going are available in real time and are far more specific and actionable. But even the best information is constrained by something more basic than quality. It is constrained by the amount of attention available to interpret it. That limit, and what it costs the company as it grows, is the subject of the next chapter.

3

The Founder's Bandwidth Is the Company's Strategic Ceiling

What built your company can now be what's blocking it — act before it costs you.

I know the exact moment the ceiling appeared in my own business. I did not recognize it as a ceiling at the time. I recognized it as an unusually busy quarter.

The company was performing well by every financial measure I tracked. Revenue was growing at 15 percent. The team was energized. We had just closed a meaningful new customer. On paper, the business was in its best condition in years. In practice, I had not had a single uninterrupted hour to think seriously about the company's strategic direction in four months.

Every morning arrived already loaded with operating demands. Every afternoon was consumed by management issues that had built up since the previous afternoon. The strategic plan we had developed at the annual offsite was sitting in a folder on my desk, its initiatives untouched and its opportunities unpursued. I was running the company. I was not leading it. That distinction, which I had understood for years in theory, had become an everyday reality I could no longer manage around.

I was 52 years old and I had built a company from nothing. I had made every important decision for more than a decade. The company had grown because of that concentrated authority. And it was now beginning to stall, not in spite of that authority, but because of it.

In the years since, as a principal investor and operating advisor working with founder led companies across several sectors, I have seen this pattern with striking regularity. The founders I sit with are not less capable than I was. They are not less committed or less strategic. They are doing exactly what produced their success at precisely the moment when doing exactly that has become the main constraint on the company's next phase of growth.

This article is about that constraint: what it is, how it forms, what it costs, and, most importantly, what can be done about it before it becomes the ceiling that limits the company's full potential.

How the Ceiling Forms

Founder-lead companies tend to move through three distinct phases of growth, and each phase makes different demands on the founder.

In the first phase, usually from inception through about $15 million in revenue, the founder is the company. Every important decision, every major customer relationship, and every serious operating problem runs through a single point of human judgment. That concentration of authority is not a flaw. It is often the source of the company's speed, coherence, and responsiveness. The founder's direct involvement is precisely what makes the company more nimble than larger and more bureaucratic competitors.

In the second phase, often between $15 million and $40 million, the founder begins to delegate, but not fully. The team grows. Functional managers are hired. Responsibility is distributed on paper. But the founder's instincts, shaped by years of being the decision maker, keep pulling him back into the details. Meetings that should be led by managers are still led by the founder. Problems that should be solved by the team are still solved by the founder. The organization learns, rationally, that escalating to the founder is the fastest path to resolution. That dynamic quietly prevents the management depth the business now needs.

In the third phase, usually above $40 million, the company requires something the founder has never had to build before: an organizational system that produces reliable outcomes without depending on the founder's direct involvement. The company is now too large for one person's judgment to serve as the main quality control mechanism. Operating complexity has exceeded the founder's processing capacity. The strategic work that will shape the company's next decade is being crowded out by the operating work the founder's continued presence keeps generating.

Most founders arrive at this stage without realizing they have crossed into it. They experience it not as a structural transition but as an unusually demanding period. The right response, which is to build the management depth and organizational systems that reduce dependence on the founder, feels like work for later. The wrong response, which is to work harder and stay deeper in the details, feels like what the moment demands.

The founder who works harder to manage the complexity of a Phase 3 company is not solving the problem. He is financing it. Every hour he spends solving an operating problem his management team should own is an hour not spent on the strategic work that will determine the company's value five years from now.

Phase	Typical Revenue Range	Founder's Role	Primary Risk
Phase 1	$0 to $15M	Operator	The founder is doing everything, which is efficient early but difficult to scale.
Phase 2	$15M to $40M	Manager	Delegation begins, but the founder stays too deep in day to day decisions.
Phase 3	$40M and above	Leader	The company needs systems and management depth that no longer rely on founder intervention.

What the Ceiling Costs

The costs of the founder bandwidth ceiling rarely show up clearly in the financial statements, which is exactly why the problem can persist for so long. They appear instead in a few operating patterns that become obvious once you know what to look for.

The first pattern is what I call the *half-started initiative*. Every founder-led company operating above its bandwidth ceiling has a set of strategic initiatives that were approved, discussed at the offsite, assigned to a team, and then left to drift for three to six months with little real progress. They are not formally canceled. They are simply crowded out by the operating demands that arrive every morning and displace the strategic work that was supposed to happen later in the day.

The second pattern is the *deferred decision*. I often ask founders to describe the most important decision they have been meaning to make for more than ninety days and still have not made. Every founder has at least one. Usually, they have several. The logic is consistent: the decision matters enough to require careful thought, which means it cannot be made in the ten minutes between calls. It needs a half day of uninterrupted attention. That half day never arrives.

The third pattern is *management arrested development*. When the founder is always present to solve the problems that arise, the management team never develops the independent problem-solving capacity a larger company requires. The team is not incapable. It is waiting, rationally, for the founder to solve what the founder has always solved. The founder, equally rationally, steps in because waiting for the team to develop new capability takes longer than handling the issue himself. Both behaviors make sense individually. Together they create an organization that cannot function at the level its growth now demands.

There is a fourth cost that founders tend to confront only when they sit across the table from a sophisticated buyer or private equity investor. *Person-dependent performance*, meaning results driven mainly by the founder's presence, relationships, and judgment rather than by durable organizational systems, is structurally less valuable than process dependent performance. A buyer purchasing EBITDA that depends on the founder staying in the business for three years is buying a less valuable asset than one purchasing EBITDA produced by a management system that can operate without the founder. The bandwidth ceiling, left unaddressed, becomes a discount embedded in the exit price.

Working harder doesn't solve complexity. It just makes the founder the system.

Example One

The Cost of the Last Decision

One of the clearest illustrations I have encountered of the bandwidth ceiling involved a founder in the industrial services sector whose company had reached 60 million dollars in annual revenue entirely on the strength of his personal judgment and direct involvement. He was, by any measure, an exceptional operator. He understood the business at every level — the customer relationships, the field operations, the equipment, the pricing dynamics of every contract the company held. He was also, by the time I engaged with him, the reason the company had stopped growing.

Every significant decision routed through him. Estimating approvals, customer escalations, hiring above a certain level, capital expenditures, contract terms — all of it landed on his desk because that was the system that had always worked. What had changed was the scale. At 60 million dollars, the volume of decisions requiring his attention had grown to the point that nothing moved quickly and the management team had learned not to act without him. Growth had stalled for eighteen months.

He made two hires: a strong operating manager with industrial services experience at comparable scale, and a CFO who had taken a similar business through a growth phase. He forced himself to stay out of the decisions he had just delegated. Revenue reached one hundred million dollars within two years.

The business had not changed. The bandwidth had.

Step	What to Do	What It Usually Reveals
1. Inventory responsibilities	List every recurring decision, meeting, escalation point, and relationship you still manage personally.	The founder is carrying more live responsibilities than he has ever formally acknowledged.
2. Estimate real time use	Calculate the weekly hours these responsibilities actually consume.	The total usually exceeds sustainable leadership capacity.
3. Identify what only you can do	Separate genuine founder only work from work that is transferable with the right capability and preparation.	Only a small fraction of the list truly requires the founder's direct involvement.

The Bandwidth Calculation

The most useful step I have learned to take with a founder facing this pattern is to make the bandwidth problem explicit before discussing solutions. The bandwidth calculation is a simple exercise any founder can complete in an afternoon, and the result is usually more revealing than expected.

First, make a complete inventory of every management responsibility you currently hold. Not the responsibilities shown on the organization chart, but the real ones. List every recurring decision you make, every recurring meeting you lead or are expected to attend, every operating issue for which you are the default escalation point, and every important relationship with customers, suppliers, lenders, or directors that you still manage personally. Most founders have never written the full list down. It is usually longer than they expect.

Second, estimate how much time each responsibility consumes in a normal week. Not how much time it should take, but how much time it does take. In almost every case I have worked through, the sum of those hours exceeds the number of hours available in a sustainable leadership week. Founders who do the exercise honestly often discover they are operating at 130 to 150 percent of realistic management capacity. That is why every day feels like an emergency. Structurally, every day is one.

Third, ask the diagnostic question that matters most: which of these responsibilities can only be performed by me? Not which do I like to do. Not which do I do best. Which ones genuinely require my specific judgment, relationships, or authority and cannot be transferred to someone else with the right capability and preparation. In my experience, that list is usually only three to five responsibilities. Everything else is transferable in principle.

The gap between the full inventory and those few truly non transferable items is the strategic ceiling. It is the management bandwidth currently being consumed by work that does not require the founder's direct involvement and that, if freed, would create room for the strategic work that determines the company's next phase of growth.

The bandwidth calculation is not a time management exercise. It is a strategic asset identification exercise. The management capacity the founder frees by addressing this ceiling is not leisure time. It is one of the company's most important strategic resources, and it is often tied up in tasks the organization should be able to perform without him.

Example Two

When the Founder Is the Bottleneck on Both Sides

The second situation I want to describe involved a fabrication company at 35 million dollars in annual revenue whose founder had built the business on two personal strengths: his ability to sell and his exacting standard for production quality. Both strengths were real. Both had become organizational liabilities.

Because he was the primary relationship holder for the company's largest accounts, the sales effort was bounded by the hours he could give it. Because his quality standard was personal rather than institutional, production supervisors deferred to him on every non-routine decision rather than developing the judgment to resolve issues independently. He was simultaneously managing customer relationships, walking the production floor, and running the business. None of the three was getting his full attention. Profitability had been flat for two years despite adequate revenue, because the organizational friction of routing everything through one person was consuming margin as surely as any cost line in the financial statements.

The change he made was structural and, by his own description, painful. He hired a General Manager with manufacturing operations experience — someone who had run a comparable facility and who could own the production environment completely. He stepped back from the floor. The sales capacity he recovered went directly into the accounts the business had been unable to develop.

Profitability improved 30 percent within 18 months. The constraint had never been the market. It had been the organization chart.

Three Actions Before Any New Strategic Priority

The bandwidth calculation identifies the problem. The next step is to address it with discipline. In practice, that means applying three actions at the same time, because the bandwidth problem compounds across all three dimensions and partial solutions rarely hold for long.

Subtract Before You Add

This is the discipline founders resist most because it feels like contraction. Before taking on any new strategic initiative, before adding any new meeting, any new customer relationship, or any new responsibility to the calendar, remove something that is already there.

The most practical version of this is a 30 day moratorium. For 30 days, the founder accepts no new operating responsibility. He joins no new recurring meetings. He takes no customer call that a senior sales or account manager can handle. He does not solve any operating problem that appears on the management team's agenda. This is not abdication. It is a diagnostic period that reveals what the organization can and cannot manage without his intervention.

The moratorium almost always reveals two things at once. First, the organization is often more capable than the founder believed. Many of the issues he has been solving were solvable by the team and were being escalated only because he had made escalation the path of least resistance. Second, the organization does have real capability gaps in a few functions or decision areas. Once identified clearly, those gaps can be addressed through focused hiring or targeted development instead of permanent founder involvement.

Institutionalize Before You Delegate

This discipline addresses the most common failure mode in founder delegation: handing off responsibility before converting the founder's tacit knowledge into an explicit process the organization can actually use.

Founders carry an enormous amount of operating knowledge in their heads. They know the criteria they use in pricing decisions, the signals they read when evaluating a new hire, and the exact steps they follow in a difficult customer situation. That knowledge was never documented because it never needed to be. The founder was always present to apply it. When a responsibility is delegated without translating that judgment into process, the new owner usually performs the work at a meaningfully lower level, the founder steps back in to correct the output, and the delegation quietly fails.

The institutionalization work is where founders most often underinvest. It takes time. It produces results with a lag. But it is the only path that creates durable capability transfer instead of temporary relief followed by reversion.

Hire for Where You Are Going, Not Where You Have Been

The third discipline is the management investment founders most often get wrong. A company that has grown from $5 million to $40 million under a founder's direct leadership usually has a team hired to execute the founder's decisions, not to make independent decisions of their own. These people may be loyal and capable. They may even have been exactly right for the company that existed two years ago. They are often not the right team for the company that needs to exist two years from now.

The investment I recommend is targeted and non negotiable: hire an A player into the two or three roles most critical to the strategic priorities that define the company's next chapter. Do not hire a cheaper B player who will require two years of development before producing independent results. Hire someone who has already operated at the level the company now needs, in a comparable setting, and who can produce independent results almost immediately.

This is almost always more expensive than founders expect and faster paying than founders expect. The management bandwidth it frees, the hours of founder attention released when a genuinely capable executive is leading a function that previously required daily founder involvement, is worth far more than the salary differential between an A player and a B player.

Freed bandwidth isn't spare time. It's the capacity to build what's next.

The Ceiling Becomes the Launchpad

The founder's bandwidth ceiling is not a personal weakness. It is the structural consequence of building a company in the most effective early stage way possible, by personally managing the decisions that matter most, holding the relationships that drive the business, and serving as the source of judgment that makes the organization work. That approach builds the company. At a certain scale, it also limits it.

What this chapter describes is not a problem solved by better prioritization or longer hours. It is a structural condition that can change only when the founder changes what the founder does, by subtracting before adding, by transferring real authority, and by building organizational capability that is no longer bounded by one person's time. The question that follows is what kind of growth that newly freed capacity is actually producing. Revenue can rise while value declines. The next chapter examines that distinction through the one metric most CEOs still underweight, return on invested capital.

4

Growing Revenue While Shrinking Value

GROWING REVENUE ISN'T THE SAME AS GROWING VALUE, FIX IT BEFORE SOMEONE ELSE NOTICES.

The ROIC Problem Most CEOs Ignore

I sat across the table from a founder three years ago who had built something that, on the surface, looked like an unqualified success story. His company had grown from $12 million to $38 million in revenue over five years. The compound annual growth rate was something his banker cited in conversation and his accountant referenced in holiday letters. He was proud of it, and he had every right to be.

He was sitting across from me because he had just received a preliminary valuation from a prospective buyer that was, in his words, insulting. He had expected a multiple commensurate with his revenue growth. The buyer had offered a multiple commensurate with his earnings quality and capital efficiency, which were significantly less impressive than his top line story suggested.

I spent the next three hours showing him something that his accountant, his banker, and his own management reporting had never shown him: his company had been growing revenue while simultaneously consuming capital faster than it was generating returns on it. For five years, every dollar of revenue growth had required more invested capital than it had returned in after tax operating profit. The business was, by the only measure that determines what a company is actually worth to a buyer, getting less valuable as it got larger.

He had been measuring the wrong thing. Not because he was unsophisticated or inattentive. Because nobody had ever told him that there was another thing to measure.

That conversation has repeated itself, in different industries and different cities, more times than I can count. The metric that most founders use to evaluate their company's performance, revenue growth, is a necessary but completely insufficient indicator of value creation. It tells you how much the company's top line is growing. It tells you nothing about whether the growth is creating or destroying the value the owner believes he is building.

Founders track growth. Buyers calculate return on capital. The gap between those two numbers is where deals fall apart.

The Illusion That Revenue Creates Value

Let me describe the mechanism through which a growing company destroys value, because it is counterintuitive enough that it requires a specific illustration to make it real.

Imagine a distribution company generating $20 million in revenue with $2 million in operating profit. To grow to $30 million in revenue, the company needs to add a warehouse, hire a sales team, build a larger inventory position, and extend more credit to the new customers it is acquiring. The capital required to support the growth, the warehouse investment, the working capital, the accounts receivable expansion, totals $6 million.

At $30 million in revenue, the operating profit has grown to $2.7 million. On paper, the company looks better: more revenue, more profit. In reality, the company has deployed $6 million of additional capital to generate $700,000 of additional annual operating profit. The return on that incremental capital investment is less than 12 percent. If the company's cost of capital is fifteen percent, a reasonable estimate for a private company at this size and risk level, the growth has destroyed value. The company is larger and worth less per dollar of capital deployed than it was before the growth occurred.

This is not a hypothetical. I have seen it in manufacturing companies, service businesses, distribution operations, and technology enabled services. The sector changes. The mechanism is the same. Growth that consumes capital faster than it generates returns on that capital is not a path to a more valuable company. It is a path to a larger company that is worth less, proportionally, than the smaller one it came from.

The founder in my opening story was not running a bad business. His operations were competent, his customers were loyal, and his team was capable. His problem was that he had never been forced to answer the question that every dollar of growth implicitly asks: what return is this capital generating relative to what it costs to deploy?

What ROIC Actually Means, in Language That Does Not Require a Finance Degree

Return on Invested Capital, or ROIC, is a phrase that appears frequently in the financial press and in the annual reports of large public companies. It rarely appears in the management discussions of mid-sized private companies, which is one of the reasons those companies consistently underperform the value creation potential of their underlying businesses. Let me translate it into operational terms.

ROIC asks a single question: for every dollar of capital put to work in this business, including owner equity, bank debt, retained earnings, and working capital, how many cents of after tax operating profit does the business generate each year?

ROIC: The Calculation in Plain Terms
ROIC = NOPAT ÷ Invested Capital
NOPAT = operating profit × (1 minus tax rate) | Invested Capital = equity + interest bearing debt, excess cash

If the business generates $2 million in after tax operating profit on $10 million of invested capital, the ROIC is 20 percent. If the cost of that capital, the blended rate the business must earn to justify the risk its investors and lenders are taking, is 13 percent, the business is creating 7 percentage points of value spread every year. It is earning more on its capital than it costs to deploy that capital. It is building genuine wealth.

If the same business generates $2 million in after tax operating profit on $20 million of invested capital, the ROIC is 10 percent. Against the same 13 percent cost of capital, the business is destroying 3 percentage points of value every year. It is earning less on its capital than it costs to deploy. The owner is working hard, growing revenue, and building something that is systematically less valuable than the capital he has put into it.

The distance between these two scenarios is not the operating profit. It is the capital efficiency, how much capital is required to generate the operating profit. This is the dimension of business performance that revenue growth, gross margin, and EBITDA, the metrics most founders track most closely, do not measure. It is also the dimension that determines, above all others, what a sophisticated buyer will pay for the business.

Growth tells you which direction you're moving. ROIC tells you whether you're building anything worth owning.

Why Founders Miss This, and Why That Is Understandable

I want to be honest about something before I explain what founders should do differently. The fact that most mid-sized company founders do not track ROIC or think explicitly about the relationship between growth and capital returns is not a failure of financial sophistication. It is the entirely predictable result of the management environment most founders operate in.

Founders build their companies in an environment where the external pressure points are revenue based. Their bankers measure covenant compliance against revenue and EBITDA. Their accountants report on revenue growth and profit margins. Their investors, if they have them, celebrate revenue milestones. Their management teams are compensated on revenue targets. The entire external financial ecosystem that surrounds a mid-sized private company is oriented toward the top line and the immediate profit margin. ROIC is not in any of these conversations because it requires a calculation that the standard management reporting package does not produce.

There is also a timing problem. ROIC erosion is slow. A company that is deploying capital inefficiently does not see the consequences in its monthly financial statements. It sees healthy revenue growth. It sees acceptable EBITDA margins. The capital efficiency problem shows up only when the company tries to raise capital, refinance its debt, or sell, moments when an outside party applies the analytical lens that the management team has never applied to its own business.

By the time the founder is sitting across from a buyer who has just told him his company is worth significantly less than he expected, the capital efficiency problem has typically been compounding for three to five years. The gap between what he believes his company is worth and what the buyer is prepared to pay is not the result of a single bad decision. It is the accumulated result of a management philosophy that optimized for top line growth without accounting for the capital cost of achieving it.

What Founders Typically Track	What Determines Enterprise Value
Revenue growth rate year over year	ROIC relative to cost of capital, is the business creating or destroying value?
Gross margin percentage	Capital efficiency, how much invested capital does each dollar of operating profit require?
EBITDA in absolute dollars	Free cash flow conversion, what percentage of EBITDA becomes cash the owner can actually deploy?
Headcount and operational scale	Working capital intensity, how much working capital is consumed per dollar of revenue growth?
New customer acquisition	Net revenue retention, is the existing customer base expanding or contracting independently of new sales?
Revenue per employee	Return on incremental capital, what does each new growth investment return relative to what it costs?

The Value Spread: The Number That Changes the Conversation

There is a number I calculate in the first month of every advisory engagement, and whose result almost always produces a significant shift in how the founder thinks about his business. I call it the value spread. It is the simplest expression of whether a company is creating or destroying value.

The Value Spread
Value Spread = ROIC minus WACC
WACC = weighted average cost of capital | Positive spread = value creation | Negative spread = value destruction

When the value spread is positive, when the business earns more on its capital than it costs to deploy, every dollar of growth creates additional value. When the value spread is negative, when the business earns less than its cost of capital, every dollar of growth destroys value. The company gets larger, but it gets less valuable per dollar of capital deployed.

For a typical mid-sized private company, the cost of capital, the WACC, is approximately 12 to 15 percent, reflecting the blended cost of bank debt, any equity investment, and the opportunity cost of the owner's retained capital. A business generating an ROIC of 18 percent has a positive value spread of 3 to 6 percent. A business generating an ROIC of 10 percent has a negative value spread of 2 to 5 percent. The difference in enterprise value between these two companies, holding everything else constant, is substantial and directly visible to any sophisticated buyer who calculates it.

What makes this particularly important for founders is the compounding effect. A company with a consistent positive value spread does not just maintain its value relative to invested capital. It builds value at a rate that exceeds the cost of its capital every year.

After five years of compound positive spread, the enterprise value premium relative to a company with a neutral or negative spread is enormous. The most common outcome I see when I calculate value spreads for companies that have been growing for five or more years is that the company's potential value, what it would be worth if it were generating a market appropriate return on its capital, is significantly higher than its current value. The gap represents the founder's unrealized wealth.

The value spread is the most important number in your business — and the one you've probably never calculated.

The Three Operational Drivers of ROIC in a Mid Sizedd Company

ROIC is not a strategic concept disconnected from daily operational decisions. It is the financial output of three specific categories of operational behavior that every founder and CEO controls directly. Understanding which operational lever has the greatest impact on ROIC at any given stage of the company's development is the practical translation of the concept into action.

Driver 1: Operating Margin

The numerator of the ROIC calculation is after tax operating profit. Every percentage point of operating margin improvement, holding capital deployment constant, improves ROIC by a corresponding amount. For a Mid-Sized company, the margin levers most directly within management control are pricing discipline, product and customer mix management, and overhead cost structure relative to revenue scale.

Pricing discipline is the most consistently underutilized margin lever in Mid-Sized companies. Research across thousands of mid-sized businesses shows that the average company is pricing below what the market will support relative to the value it delivers by a meaningful amount, not because its products or services are commoditized, but because pricing decisions are made by salespeople whose incentives reward volume rather than margin, and whose discomfort with price resistance leads them to offer discounts that are not necessary to win the business.

A one percentage point improvement in operating margin on $30 million of revenue is $300,000 of additional annual operating profit. On a $12 million invested capital base, that single improvement increases ROIC by 2.5 percentage points. The cumulative effect on enterprise value, capitalized at a market rate, is between $1.5 million and $2.5 million in additional value created without a dollar of additional revenue.

Driver 2: Capital Efficiency

The denominator of the ROIC calculation is invested capital. Every dollar of capital consumed by the business that does not generate a proportional return reduces ROIC and destroys value. The three most significant capital efficiency levers for mid-sized companies are working capital management, capital expenditure discipline, and asset utilization.

Working capital is where most mid-sized company capital efficiency losses originate. Accounts receivable that are not collected on the terms agreed. Inventory that accumulates beyond the level required to support sales. Payables that are paid faster than necessary because no one is systematically managing the terms. Each of these dynamics consumes capital that is not generating a return, effectively increasing the denominator of the ROIC calculation without increasing the numerator.

A company that reduces its cash conversion cycle, the number of days between paying for its inputs and collecting from its customers, by fifteen days frees a significant amount of capital from working capital deployment. On a $30 million revenue business, a fifteen day reduction in the cash conversion cycle releases approximately $1.2 million of previously trapped capital. That capital can be returned to the owner, deployed in genuinely value creating investments, or used to reduce the debt whose interest cost is embedded in the WACC calculation.

Driver 3: Revenue Quality and Sustainability

The third ROIC driver is less intuitively connected to the formula but is equally important to the enterprise value conclusion: the predictability and sustainability of the revenue that the capital is deployed to generate.

Two companies can have identical ROIC calculations and meaningfully different enterprise values if one's revenue is contracted, recurring, and customer diversified, while the other's is transactional, project based, and concentrated in three accounts. The capital required to generate the revenue may be similar. The confidence a sophisticated buyer has that the revenue will continue to be generated, and therefore that the ROIC will continue to be earned, is not similar at all. Revenue quality is the insurance policy on the ROIC calculation.

ROIC Driver	Operational Lever	Management Practice Required
Operating Margin	Pricing discipline	Annual pricing review; market rate analysis; elimination of unnecessary discount authority at sales level
Operating Margin	Product and customer mix	80/20 analysis of margin by product and customer; systematic defunding of low margin activity
Capital Efficiency	Working capital cycle	Days sales outstanding tracking; inventory turn targets; payables terms management
Capital Efficiency	CapEx discipline	Explicit return threshold for all capital investments; post investment return review
Revenue Sustainability	Recurring revenue conversion	Contractualization of key accounts; shift from transactional to retainer or subscription models where viable
Revenue Sustainability	Customer concentration management	Active new account development to reduce top customer concentration below 20 percent

How Founders and CEOs Can Incorporate This Into Their Planning and Operations

The practical challenge for a mid-sized company founder who has not previously tracked ROIC is that the concept, while straightforward in principle, requires a calculation that the standard management reporting package does not produce. Closing that gap requires five specific actions, each of which is achievable without a sophisticated financial infrastructure and none of which requires hiring a CFO, engaging a financial consultant, or implementing new software.

PRACTICE 1: CALCULATE YOUR ROIC AND VALUE SPREAD TODAY

Before any planning discussion about growth, calculate your current ROIC. You need three numbers: your most recent twelve months of operating profit; your effective tax rate; and your total invested capital (equity plus interest bearing debt minus cash). Calculate the first two into NOPAT, then divide NOPAT by invested capital. Compare the result to your estimated cost of capital, for most mid-size private companies, 12 to 15 percent is an appropriate starting range. The gap between your ROIC and your cost of capital is your current value spread. If it is positive, your growth is creating value. If it is negative or close to zero, you need to understand why before you commit to a growth plan that will compound the problem.

PRACTICE 2: ADD ROIC TO YOUR MONTHLY MANAGEMENT REPORTING

ROIC should appear in your monthly management reporting alongside revenue, gross margin, and EBITDA. Not as an academic exercise but as a management accountability metric. Specifically: track ROIC on a trailing twelve month basis, updated monthly. Track the value spread alongside it. And track the three sub components, operating margin, working capital days, and asset utilization, that explain whether ROIC is improving or deteriorating. When the management team sees ROIC monthly, the conversations that follow naturally improve capital allocation decisions. Managers begin to think about the capital cost of the resources they are requesting, not just the revenue they expect those resources to generate.

PRACTICE 3: EVALUATE EVERY GROWTH INVESTMENT THROUGH AN ROIC LENS

Before committing to any significant growth investment, a new market, a new product line, a capacity expansion, a major hire, calculate the expected return on the incremental capital the investment requires. Specifically: how much capital, in total, will this investment deploy over the next three years? What operating profit, after the investment has fully ramped, will it generate? What is the expected ROIC on the incremental investment, and does it exceed your current cost of capital? A growth investment that is expected to generate an incremental ROIC above your cost of capital is genuinely value creating. One that is not is the mechanism through which companies grow revenue while destroying value.

PRACTICE 4: USE ROIC AS A STRATEGIC FILTER

In your annual strategic planning process, evaluate every strategic priority through the ROIC lens before it is approved. Not as a replacement for the qualitative strategic assessment, competitive positioning, market opportunity, capability alignment, but as a financial discipline that prevents the approval of growth strategies whose capital economics are fundamentally unattractive. Ask explicitly: what is the expected ROIC of this strategic initiative at maturity? How does that compare to our current ROIC and our cost of capital? What would need to be true for this initiative to be value creating rather than value destroying? The answers to these questions do not always prevent a strategic initiative from being approved. But they ensure that the strategic discussion is grounded in the financial reality that will eventually determine what the initiative is worth.

PRACTICE 5: TIE MANAGEMENT COMPENSATION TO ROIC IMPROVEMENT

Revenue based management incentives produce revenue based management behavior. If the management team is compensated on revenue growth, managers will pursue revenue growth regardless of its capital efficiency. Adding an ROIC component to the management incentive plan, even a modest one, representing 20 to 30 percent of the variable compensation structure, changes the management conversation about growth in a measurable way. Managers begin to evaluate growth opportunities through a capital efficiency lens because their compensation depends on it. Over time, this behavioral change produces a management culture that naturally generates the capital discipline that ROIC improvement requires.

What Changes When a Buyer Looks at Your Business

Every sophisticated buyer I have been on the same side of the table as, private equity firms, strategic acquirors, family offices, growth capital investors, calculates ROIC as part of their initial evaluation of an acquisition target. They may not always use that exact term. They calculate it, they calculate the value spread, and they form a view about whether the company's current capital deployment is creating or destroying value. That view directly affects what they are willing to pay.

The companies that achieve the highest transaction multiples are not always the ones growing fastest. They are the ones whose ROIC is above their cost of capital and improving. A company growing at 12 percent per year with a value spread of 6 percentage points is consistently worth more at the transaction table than one growing at

18 percent with a value spread of negative 2 percentage points. The faster growing company looks more impressive on the revenue line. The more capital efficient company is demonstrably building more wealth per dollar of capital deployed, which is the only definition of value creation that determines what a buyer will actually pay.

This matters practically because it changes the conversation a founder should be having with himself about the relationship between growth and value creation. Growth is not the enemy of ROIC. Growth pursued with capital discipline, with explicit attention to the return each incremental investment generates, is the most powerful value creator available to a mid-sized company founder. Growth pursued without that discipline is the mechanism through which ambitious, hardworking founders build companies that are worth less than the effort and capital they have invested in them.

I want to return to the founder I described at the beginning. After our three hour conversation, he spent six months working through the ROIC analysis for every segment of his business. He identified the three product lines that were generating ROIC above his cost of capital. He identified the two that were not. He restructured the pricing on one and eliminated the other. He reduced his cash conversion cycle by eighteen days through disciplined receivables management. He implemented a capital return threshold for all new growth investments.

Two years later, revenue had grown by a modest eight percent. ROIC had increased from nine percent to seventeen percent. The value spread had moved from negative four percentage points to positive four. A second buyer evaluated the business and offered forty percent more than the first.

The business had not fundamentally changed. Its competitive position was similar, its customer base was similar, and its management team was the same. What had changed was its capital efficiency, the return it was generating on every dollar its owner had put to work. That change, and nothing else, was responsible for the entire difference in valuation.

Don't grow faster. Grow in a way that creates more value than it consumes.

Summary

Revenue growth is the number most founders track with the greatest emotion, and for understandable reasons. It is the visible proof that the company is moving.

What this chapter examines is the relationship between growth and value creation, and the conditions under which the two separate. A business can grow revenue by deploying capital at returns below its cost and destroy value while still looking successful on the surface. ROIC is not a finance department abstraction. It is a practical lens that shows whether the growth being pursued is worth the capital it consumes.

Complexity, information quality, founder bandwidth, and capital return are not separate management topics. They form the operating base on which strategy is built. The next chapter turns to strategy directly and asks what happens when the plan begins with the right diagnostic question and what happens when it does not

5

Most Strategic Plans Are Goal Lists Wearing the Clothes of Strategy

A PLAN THAT DOESN'T GET EXECUTED ISN'T A STRATEGY, HERE'S WHAT ACTUALLY CLOSES THAT GAP.

Every year the same ritual unfolds. A management team gathers. An offsite is scheduled. Slides are built. Over one or two days the team talks about where the company has been and where it should go. The result is a strategic plan.

The document usually looks complete. It has a vision statement, a mission statement, a set of strategic priorities, supporting initiatives, and a financial projection that shows revenue rising and margins expanding over the next three years. Everyone who helped produce it feels good about it. The CEO presents it to the board with confidence.

Six months later the document is in a folder and the initiatives are still largely unstarted. Operational demands have taken over. The management team has not returned to the strategy in any serious way since the retreat ended. The company is running on the same logic it used before the plan was produced, now with one additional burden: a set of commitments no one is actually managing.

I have seen this pattern too many times to treat it as unusual. I have seen it in companies I ran, before I understood why it was happening. I have seen it in companies I chaired, and in companies I invested in and advised. Strategic planning failure is not rare. It is the norm.

The reason is almost always the same. The plan is a goal list dressed up as strategy. It describes where the company wants to go without honestly diagnosing where the company is, why it is there, and what specific obstacles stand between the current position and the future being projected. It is built on aspiration rather than analysis, and on hope rather than facts.

A strategy without honest diagnosis isn't a strategy. It's a wish list with a timeline.

The Disease and Its Symptoms

The failure is not a failure of intelligence or commitment. The founders and CEOs I work with are capable, experienced, and genuinely motivated to grow their companies. The failure is structural, it is embedded in what the planning process leaves out.

A respected planning expert's, Richard Rumelt, distinction is useful here. A real strategy has three elements: a diagnosis of the challenge, a guiding policy for addressing it, and a set of coherent actions that follow from that policy. A goal list has none of this. It has objectives and targets, but it avoids the hard work of diagnosis and the trade offs that strategy demands.

The symptoms of plan failure are remarkably consistent. I look for them in every company I advise because they almost always point to the same result: a document that does not produce organizational change.

Symptom	What It Signals
The plan has more than five strategic priorities	The team did not make the difficult choices about what matters most. Everything is a priority, which means nothing is.
The projections improve steadily across all three years	The plan was built around a desired outcome rather than a realistic view of what the current position and constraints make possible.
The strategy does not eliminate any current activity	No real trade offs were made. The plan adds work without subtracting anything, even though the organization is already at capacity.
No single individual owns each major initiative	The plan was produced by a committee and assigned to a committee. Shared accountability becomes no accountability.
The new plan looks almost identical to last year's	The company updated the numbers without reexamining the underlying logic.
The plan is not reviewed in monthly management meetings	Strategy and operations have been separated. The document exists, but it is not being used as a management tool.

The strongest signal of all requires no document. Ask each member of the leadership team the same question: what are the two or three most important things the company must get right in the next twelve months for the business to be materially stronger than it is today? In most companies, the answers differ sharply from person to person. Different priorities. Different timeframes. Different assumptions about what the real challenge is.

When a leadership team cannot agree on the company's central challenge, the planning process does not resolve the disagreement. It aggregates it. The resulting document names several directions at once and calls that strategy. The organization then continues pulling in multiple directions, exactly as it did before the plan was written.

Why mid-sized Companies Are Especially Vulnerable

This failure is not unique to mid-sized companies, but it is especially damaging there. Large corporations have strategy teams, analysts, and planners whose full time job is to gather market intelligence, benchmark performance, and challenge assumptions. mid-sized companies usually have none of this.

In most mid-sized companies, the CEO and CFO are the planning function. The competitive perspective they bring into the offsite is whatever they have gathered while also running the business. The outside perspective that might challenge the company's assumptions is usually absent.

The founder also faces a second constraint. He is often both the chief strategist and the primary operating manager. Strategic thinking requires protected time. In most mid-sized companies that time does not really exist, except for a day or two at an offsite.

The result is predictable: a planning process compressed in time, thin in external perspective, and dominated by the CEO's existing mental model of the business. The document that emerges is often not a strategy. It is a formalization of what the CEO already believed, decorated with contributions from the team and packaged in the language of planning.

Most strategic plans are just the CEO's existing beliefs, dressed up to look like strategy.

Diagnosis First

The single change that most reliably improves the quality of a strategic planning process is also the one most often skipped: an honest, specific, externally informed diagnosis of the company's current competitive situation before any discussion of where the company should go.

I use the word diagnosis deliberately. A doctor who skips the examination and goes directly to the prescription is guessing.

A management team that jumps into strategic objectives before examining its actual position, operating weaknesses, and market dynamics is doing the same thing.

This diagnosis is not a superficial SWOT exercise. In practice, most SWOT sessions turn into a polite confirmation of what management already believes. Strengths are overstated. Weaknesses are softened. Opportunities are optimistic. Threats are noted and discounted.

The diagnosis that matters answers a harder question: what is the most important thing that is true about our competitive situation right now that we are not fully acknowledging in the way we run this business?

That question requires setting aside the company's internal narrative and looking at the evidence with outside eyes. It requires customer interviews that are not curated, competitive intelligence that is not filtered through optimism, and financial analysis that looks for what the numbers are concealing rather than what they confirm.

In my experience, one of the most useful diagnostic questions is this: if our best customer were deciding whether to stay with us or move to our strongest competitor, what would be the three strongest arguments in the competitor's favor? Not the arguments the sales team handles every day. The ones that keep the CEO awake because he knows they are true.

Strategy isn't about the destination. It's about facing where you are — and choosing differently.

The Three Questions a Useful Strategic Plan Must Answer

Once the diagnosis is clear, the planning process becomes much simpler. Not easy. Simple. The complexity of strategy usually reflects incomplete diagnosis. When the diagnosis is precise, the strategic choices that follow tend to be more obvious than the planning process suggests.

A strategic plan that is genuinely useful answers three questions.

1. What specific competitive challenge are we solving?

Not the financial target we want to hit. The specific competitive or operating problem that, if solved, would produce the financial result. A company with declining margins is not facing a margin problem in the abstract. It is facing a pricing problem, a cost structure problem, or a customer mix problem. The strategic question is which one, with evidence.

2. What exactly are we going to do differently?

Not what we will continue doing, and not what we will simply do more of. What will we do differently from today? Every real strategic choice displaces something else. A plan that adds initiatives without removing activity is not a strategy. It is a workload expansion.

3. How will we know in ninety days whether it is working?

Not in three years when the projections are due. In ninety days. This question forces the plan into operating reality. It requires the team to identify the leading indicators that will move before the financial results do, and to review them on a cadence that still allows correction.

Building the Plan on Facts, Not Hope

Most financial projections in strategic plans share the same characteristic: they improve. Revenue rises. Margins expand. EBITDA grows. The trajectory is upward, and the assumptions are optimistic enough to feel plausible.

This is rarely dishonesty. It is the predictable result of a planning process that starts with the outcome the team wants and then works backward to the assumptions required to support it.

I call this hope based planning. I use the term carefully because I have produced these plans myself. When you have built a company and feel responsible for its people and future, optimism has a strong pull. But optimism is not a strategy.

The alternative is fact based planning. That does not mean pessimism. A fact based plan can still project growth and margin expansion. The difference is that its assumptions are tied to observable dynamics: customer behavior, win rates, sales cycles, retention, capacity, and the actual market share the company can reasonably capture with the resources it has.

A team that knows its realistic base case can make decisions to improve it. A team managing against an aspirational projection is not making strategic decisions. It is waiting to be surprised.

"Growth will accelerate in year two." If you can't say exactly why, that's hope, not strategy.

The Strategy on One Page

I use a simple rule in every company I advise: if the strategy cannot be stated on one page in language that every member of the management team can read in three minutes and use to make better decisions, it has not been thought through clearly enough.

This rule is not about brevity for its own sake. It is about clarity. A strategy that requires forty pages to explain often reflects choices that have not actually been made. The document's complexity becomes cover for the absence of hard decisions.

The one page strategy I use has five elements.

Element	The Question It Answers	What This Prevents
The Diagnosis	What is the specific challenge we are solving?	Initiatives that address symptoms rather than causes.
Winning Aspiration	What does winning look like in three years, specifically and measurably?	Vague goals that cannot be judged as achieved or not achieved.
Where to Play	In which markets, segments, and geographies will we compete, and which will we not?	Resource dilution across too many fronts.
How to Win	What specific advantage will allow us to win in that chosen field?	Generic positioning that could apply to any company in the sector.
Three Initiatives	What three actions will we execute in the next twelve months, with owners and milestones?	Initiative proliferation that consumes bandwidth without creating progress.

The discipline of completing this framework honestly is harder than producing a longer document. It is also faster. A team willing to face reality, make trade offs, and limit itself to three initiatives can finish a genuine strategy in two days.

The one page format also solves the communication problem. A forty page plan cannot be communicated in a way that changes behavior. A one page strategy can be reviewed at every management meeting, posted on the wall, and used as a decision filter in day to day work.

Implementation, the Part Most Teams Skip

Kaplan and Norton found that most executive teams spend less than one hour per month discussing strategy. Not results. Not budget variance. Strategy. That finding has never surprised me.

In many companies, the strategic plan is treated as a planning deliverable rather than a management tool. It is produced, approved, and then set aside while the operating calendar takes over again.

The most effective implementation architecture I have found is simple. Every monthly management meeting begins with a brief strategy review. Ten minutes is enough, if the discipline is real.

The review should answer three questions: are the three strategic initiatives on track, if not what is blocking them, and has anything changed in the market or the company's performance that requires the strategy to be reconsidered?

This short review keeps strategy visible in the same calendar where the operating decisions are made. It prevents the plan from disappearing the moment pressure rises.

> ***Strategy execution is not a project running alongside the business. It is a management discipline embedded in the operating calendar.***

The other implementation failure I see repeatedly is the absence of single person accountability. Every initiative needs one named owner. Not a team. Not a function. A person. When progress will be reviewed every month with one person accountable, execution becomes far more likely. When the initiative belongs to everyone, it usually belongs to no one.

What Changes When the Plan Is Built on Facts

The companies that build their strategic plans on honest diagnosis and factual projection do not just execute more effectively. They grow faster, generate better margins, and become more valuable when a transaction occurs.

The reason is straightforward. The same discipline that produces a better strategy also produces better operating decisions throughout the year. Teams that are honest about the company's position make better choices about where to allocate resources, what to hire for, and what customers or products deserve emphasis.

I am often asked what the return on investment of a strong strategic planning process is. My answer is that strategy and execution are not separable. A strategy that is not executed is worth nothing. An organization executing without strategic clarity is working hard in a direction that may not be right.

But I can say what I have seen in companies that get this right. They stop doing unproductive things faster. They allocate resources more effectively. They make clearer choices about what not to pursue. They arrive at capital raises, acquisitions, and exits with businesses that were run deliberately rather than opportunistically.

A sophisticated acquiror or investor sees something unusual in those businesses: an organization that knows what it is doing and why. That clarity is visible in the management presentation, in the financial results, and in the diligence process. It is worth a premium.

> ***Anyone can produce a strategic plan. The discipline of building one on honest diagnosis and factual assessment, rather than aspiration and hope, is rare. And it shows.***

Summary

The strategic plan most mid-sized companies produce is usually the document at the end of the planning process, not the expression of strategic clarity. This chapter shows the specific ways that document stops short of becoming a true strategy.

It does not diagnose why the company is not already achieving what it says it wants. It does not force the trade offs that real strategic choice requires. And it does not connect intended direction to the specific behaviors that would make execution possible. Companies that begin by asking what they want to achieve usually produce goals. Companies that begin by asking why they are not already there, and what specifically must change, are the ones that produce strategy. But even when a management team gets that part right, another problem quickly appears. The organization still wants to do too much at once.

The next chapter takes up that issue directly and argues that the number of priorities in the plan is often the single best predictor of whether any of them will actually happen.

6

The Three Initiative Rule

Unmanaged ambition doesn't multiply success, it multiplies stalled initiatives.

Why Doing Less Produces More

There is a specific kind of organizational damage that is almost impossible to diagnose while it is happening, that announces itself only after the harm is done, and that is caused almost entirely by success.

I have seen it in companies I have run and in companies I have invested in and advised. It begins with a win. The company executes something significant, a new product launch that exceeds projections, a market expansion that delivers ahead of schedule, a restructuring that produces the efficiency improvement everyone doubted was achievable. The confidence generated by that success is real and deserved. And then, in the months that follow, something happens that is invisible until it becomes undeniable.

The leadership team, energized and emboldened by the first success, launches the next initiative. And the one after that. And several more simultaneously, because the logic of the moment says: if we can do one thing well, we can do many things well. The pipeline of strategic ideas, which the previous success has validated and expanded, is now being converted into an expanding portfolio of active initiatives. Each one has a sponsor. Each one has a team. Each one appears, in isolation, achievable.

The organization does not immediately collapse under the weight. It bends. Response times slow and meetings multiply. The quality of work on each individual initiative declines as the people executing it divide their attention across three or four other priorities. Key contributors, the ones with enough capability to be assigned to multiple initiatives simultaneously, begin to look exhausted. Then they begin to look disengaged. Then, in the most costly sequence of events in organizational life, some of them begin to leave.

The leadership team, surveying a portfolio of initiatives that are all partially complete and none of which are producing the results that launched them, draws the wrong conclusion. The problem, they decide, is execution quality. They hire a program manager and implement status reporting. They hold more reviews. They are adding accountability infrastructure to an organization that does not have an accountability problem. It has a focus problem. And until they diagnose it correctly, no accountability infrastructure in the world will fix it.

Ambition scales faster than capacity. That gap is the most destructive force in a growing company.

The Success Trap: How Winning Generates Overcommitment

Let me describe the psychology of the post success overcommitment, because understanding why it happens is a prerequisite for understanding why it is so difficult to prevent.

When a company executes a significant initiative successfully, the experience produces several overlapping effects that all point in the same direction.

Confidence expands. The leadership team's estimate of what the organization is capable of rises, appropriately, based on evidence. This confidence is not misplaced. The organization did accomplish something difficult. The error is in the assumption that the same team, with the same structure and the same bandwidth, can replicate that performance simultaneously across multiple new challenges rather than sequentially across one at a time.

Ambition unlocks. Success reveals adjacencies. The market expansion that worked suggests two more market expansions. The product launch that succeeded suggests three more product opportunities. The operational improvement that produced cost savings suggests five more operational improvements. Each adjacency is real and each opportunity is legitimate. The problem is not the quality of the opportunities. It is the quantity of them being pursued simultaneously on the assumption that more attempts will produce proportionally more results.

Momentum pressure builds. Once a portfolio of initiatives is publicly announced, communicated to the management team, included in board presentations, shared with key customers or investors, there is significant social pressure against removing any of them. Each initiative has an internal sponsor whose professional commitment is attached to it. Removing an initiative from the portfolio feels like a judgment of the initiative's sponsor as much as the initiative itself. This social friction prevents the portfolio rationalization that the organization's actual capacity requires.

The combination of expanded confidence, unlocked ambition, and momentum pressure produces an initiative portfolio that consistently exceeds the organization's execution capacity. Not dramatically. Not visibly. The portfolio exceeds capacity by the kind of margin that produces chronic underdelivery on every initiative rather than catastrophic failure on any single one. This is the most organizationally damaging scenario available, because it is the one that is hardest to diagnose.

Clean failure teaches. Chronic underdelivery exhausts — and drives out the people you most need to keep.

What Initiative Overcommitment Does to an Organization

The organizational consequences of sustained initiative overcommitment are specific, predictable, and in my experience almost universally present in companies that have been running too many simultaneous strategic efforts for more than twelve months. They are also among the most difficult problems a CEO can address, because their causes are embedded in the behavior and the confidence that produced the company's success.

Symptom 1 , The Half Started Initiative Graveyard

What it looks like in the organization: The organization has a growing collection of initiatives that were launched with genuine commitment and that are now in various states of partial completion. Some are nominally active with no meaningful progress in the past quarter. Some have been quietly de prioritized without a formal decision to suspend them. Some are being maintained by a single committed individual whose team has been reassigned to newer priorities. All of them represent prior commitments that were not honored.

What it costs beyond the obvious: Beyond the wasted resources of the partial efforts themselves, the half started initiative graveyard has a specific and damaging effect on organizational culture: it teaches the management team that strategic commitments are not real commitments. When employees learn that the initiatives announced with fanfare are routinely abandoned without acknowledgment, they begin to apply the same degree of commitment to new initiatives that past experience tells them they deserve, which is minimal. The organizational cynicism generated by unfulfilled strategic commitments is among the most corrosive cultural forces in mid-sized company life, and it is entirely self inflicted.

Symptom 2 , The A Player Overallocation Problem

What it looks like in the organization: The organization's most capable people are assigned to multiple initiatives simultaneously. Each assignment is individually reasonable, these are the people most likely to succeed on each individual initiative. Collectively, the assignments exceed what any person can execute at the quality level each initiative deserves. The A players are stretched across three priorities and delivering at the level of none of them.

What it costs beyond the obvious: The A player overallocation problem has a compounding consequence that is less visible than the performance degradation itself: the best people in the organization become the most tired, the most frustrated, and the most likely to leave. The very fact of being a high performer in an overcommitted organization makes a person more miserable than being an average performer, because high performers are assigned more and held to a higher standard. The initiative overcommitment that the CEO installed in the name of growth is systematically depleting the human capital that growth requires.

Symptom 3 , Priority Ambiguity Paralysis

What it looks like in the organization: When an organization is running seven strategic initiatives simultaneously, the front line employee who faces a daily choice about where to direct her discretionary effort has no rational basis for that choice. All seven initiatives have been presented as important. All seven have sponsors at the senior level. All seven appear in the quarterly communication. None of them has been explicitly ranked against the others in a way that would give the employee a decision rule for the hundred small choices she makes each week.

What it costs beyond the obvious: Priority ambiguity does not produce random effort allocation. It produces effort allocation toward whatever generates the least management friction, the initiative whose sponsor is most present, the deliverable whose deadline is nearest, the work that is easiest to show as complete in a status report. The strategic work that is most important frequently generates the most uncertainty and requires the most sustained effort with the least visible immediate progress. In an ambiguous priority environment, that work is consistently deferred. The organization is systematically avoiding its most important work.

Symptom 4 , Morale Erosion And The Quiet Exodus

What it looks like in the organization: A management team that has been working at sustained over capacity for twelve to eighteen months begins to exhibit specific behavioral signals: a decline in the quality of contributions in management meetings; a reduction in the discretionary effort that distinguishes excellent performance from adequate performance; an increase in the frequency of sick days, personal days, and requests for schedule flexibility. These signals are the early indicators of an organizational morale problem that, if unaddressed, will produce a talent exodus in the twelve months that follow.

What it costs beyond the obvious: The people who leave first are not the weakest performers. They are the most capable, the most self aware, and the most employable, the ones who have the clearest view of the organizational dysfunction and the most options for escaping it. The organization that loses its best people to initiative overcommitment does not lose them to a competitor who offered more money. It loses them to any employer who offers them a clear priority and a realistic chance of doing one thing well. The departure of these people is not a talent management problem. It is a strategy problem wearing a talent management costume.

The Mathematics of Overcommitment

I want to make the capacity argument concrete, because it is often met with resistance by management teams who believe that running more initiatives simply requires more effort and that their organization is capable of the effort required. The mathematics do not support this belief.

A mid-sized company management team at the director level and above typically has a combined strategic work capacity, the time available for non operational, non recurring work, of approximately 40 percent of their total work hours. The remaining 60 percent is consumed by operational management: the meetings, the decisions, the communications, and the firefighting that are the daily substance of running a functioning business. This 40 percent varies by individual and by role, but it is a reasonable estimate for the aggregate strategic capacity of a management team that is also running a business.

A single well scoped strategic initiative, a new market entry, a product development effort, an operational transformation, requires approximately 15 to 20 percent of the management team's total strategic capacity to execute at the level the initiative requires. Two initiatives consume 30 to 40 percent. Three initiatives consume the entire available strategic capacity and leave no margin for the unexpected, the competitive development, the customer crisis, the operational problem, that will inevitably arise.

Above three simultaneous initiatives, the mathematics produce a predictable and consistent outcome: each additional initiative does not receive proportional additional effort. It receives attention taken from the initiatives already in the portfolio, reducing the quality and velocity of work on each of them. The management team is not making a conscious decision to underfund each initiative. They are experiencing the mechanical consequence of a portfolio that has exceeded their available capacity.

Active Initiative Count	Observed Outcomes in Organizations I Have Run or Advised
1 to 2 initiatives	Full management attention available; fast progress; high completion rate; learning applied to each subsequent effort; team energy sustained
3 initiatives	Capacity fully deployed; progress is achievable but requires discipline; no margin for the unexpected; first signs of scheduling friction in cross functional work
4 to 5 initiatives	Chronic underfunding of all initiatives; all slower than expected; status reporting proliferates to manage appearance of progress; A players begin showing stress signals
6+ initiatives	Organizational stall; most initiatives effectively on hold masked by nominal activity; morale deterioration measurable; talent attrition risk elevated; the half started initiative graveyard fills

Beyond three concurrent initiatives, every addition cuts completion odds by 15 points. At six, each one is more likely to fail than succeed.

Why Leaders Resist This Diagnosis

I have presented the overcommitment diagnosis to more management teams than I can count, and the response follows a predictable pattern. The intellectual acceptance is almost immediate. The management team recognizes the description. They have been living inside it. They can name the half started initiatives, the overallocated A players, the priority ambiguity. They nod at the mathematics.

The behavioral response is much slower, because the action that the diagnosis requires, reducing the number of active initiatives, making explicit choices about what not to pursue, publicly canceling or suspending commitments that were made with genuine conviction, runs into a set of organizational and psychological resistances that are as powerful as any financial or operational constraint.

The first resistance is the sunk cost problem. Every initiative that has been active for more than three months has consumed resources that the management team experienced as a real investment. Suspending an initiative that has consumed three months of a senior manager's time and two hundred thousand dollars of operating budget feels like writing off an investment rather than protecting the investments that remain. The sunk cost is not recoverable regardless of whether the initiative continues. But it feels recoverable, and that feeling prevents the decision.

The second resistance is the political cost of prioritization. Every initiative that is canceled or suspended has a sponsor whose professional commitment was attached to it. Making the explicit decision that Initiative B is less important than Initiative A is simultaneously a strategic decision and a statement about the relative strategic value of the people who championed each. Most leadership teams avoid explicit prioritization not because they lack the analytical capability to rank their initiatives but because they lack the political willingness to accept the personal consequences of the ranking.

The third resistance is the visibility trap. A leadership team that has publicly committed to seven initiatives and then announces that it is canceling four of them appears to have failed at four things rather than choosing to succeed at three. The optics of focused execution, to the board, to investors, to customers, to employees, are worse in the short term than the optics of ambitious overcommitment, even when the long term organizational consequences are the reverse.

I have learned, over decades of running companies and advising them, that there is only one antidote to these resistances. It is the explicit reframing of the focus decision, not as the abandonment of ambition but as the preservation of execution quality. The organization that focuses on three initiatives is not less ambitious than the one running seven. It is more likely to be ambitious next year, because it will have completed three things rather than stalled on seven.

The three initiative rule is not a formula derived from academic research. It is a management discipline I arrived at through direct operating experience and have validated through observation across dozens of mid-sized companies.

The rule is simple: at any given time, the management team has no more than three active strategic initiatives. Three initiatives that are fully resourced, explicitly prioritized, and reviewed in every management meeting. Three initiatives whose owners are named individuals who are held accountable for specific milestones in specific timeframes. Three initiatives and nothing else that claims the title of strategic priority.

The rule is not a constraint on ambition. A company that completes three well chosen strategic initiatives each year is executing at a pace that the majority of mid-sized competitors cannot match. Over five years, that cadence produces 15 completed strategic efforts, each building on the organizational learning of the ones before it. The compound effect of 15 completed initiatives, executed at high quality, is a fundamentally stronger competitive position than the compound effect of a 100 partially executed initiatives, none of which produced the outcome it was launched to achieve.

The rule is also not a permanent cap. Three is the maximum concurrent count at any moment, not the annual production target. When an initiative is completed, a new one enters the portfolio. The pipeline remains full. The organization's work is simply sequenced rather than simultaneous, and the difference in execution quality between sequenced and simultaneous work is, in my experience, the difference between an organization that feels effective and one that feels stalled.

What Counts as a Strategic Initiative

The three-initiative rule requires a clear definition of what qualifies as a strategic initiative, because the discipline only works if the portfolio is honestly counted. A strategic initiative is any effort that requires sustained cross functional management attention over more than sixty days, has a named owner at the director level or above, and is expected to produce a material change in the company's competitive position, operational capability, or financial performance.

Operational improvements that can be executed within a single function are not strategic initiatives. Customer service projects that are managed within the service function do not count. Product modifications managed within the product team do not count. What counts is the work that requires the CEO's attention, claims the discretionary time of multiple senior leaders, and competes for the management bandwidth that determines what the organization can actually accomplish.

Six Disciplines That Restore Focus to an Overcommitted Organization

The three initiative rule is the principle. The following disciplines are the practices through which it is installed and maintained in an organization that has been running too many initiatives for too long. They are presented in the sequence in which they should be implemented, because the order matters. The most difficult discipline, the initiative moratorium, must come first, because it creates the capacity for everything that follows.

Discipline 1 , The Initiative Moratorium

Before any new initiative is considered, institute a 45 day moratorium on all new strategic commitments. No new initiatives are approved, announced, or staffed during this period. The moratorium is not a retreat from ambition. It is a diagnostic period in which the management team conducts an honest audit of everything currently in the active initiative portfolio: what is actually progressing, what has stalled, what has been completed, and what should never have been started. The audit almost always reveals that the organization is working on more things than it can name and completing fewer things than it believes. The moratorium is the first honest conversation the leadership team has had about capacity in years.

Discipline 2 , The Portfolio Rationalization

Following the audit, formally rank every active initiative against two criteria: strategic importance and probability of completion with available resources. For each initiative in the portfolio, ask one question: if this is the only initiative we complete this year, will it have been worth the organizational investment? The initiatives that cannot survive this question are candidates for suspension. The portfolio rationalization is not a comfortable exercise. It requires the leadership team to make the explicit prioritization decisions that organizational politics have been deferring. It requires telling initiative sponsors that their project is not among the top three. That conversation is difficult. It is also the most important leadership act in the restoration of organizational focus.

Discipline 3 , The Three Initiative Contract

Following the portfolio rationalization, formally contract three initiatives and only three. The contract is not a planning document. It is an organizational commitment with five specific elements: a named initiative owner with line accountability for the outcome; a specific, measurable definition of what success looks like in ninety days and at twelve months; an explicit resource allocation, the specific people, budget, and management time committed to this initiative and no other competing priority; kill criteria, the specific conditions under which the initiative will be suspended rather than continued; and a review cadence, the specific meeting in the management calendar at which progress will be reviewed, in the same format, every week. These five elements distinguish a strategic commitment from a strategic aspiration. Aspirations are easy to announce and impossible to hold accountable.

Discipline 4 , The Addition Rule

Once the three initiative portfolio is established, implement a standing rule: no new initiative enters the portfolio without an existing initiative exiting it. The addition rule prevents the portfolio from expanding back to its prior overcommitted state under the pressure of new opportunities and management enthusiasm. It also forces the most important strategic question a management team can ask: is this new opportunity more important than what we are already doing? When the question is framed as a substitution rather than an addition, it receives the analytical attention it deserves. Most organizations answer 'yes' to 'should we add this?' without examining the opportunity cost. Very few answer 'yes' to 'should we stop doing that in order to do this?'

Discipline 5 , The Weekly Ten Minute Initiative Review

The three initiative portfolio must be reviewed in every weekly management meeting in a format that takes no more than 10 minutes and produces a specific output: for each initiative, is it on track, at risk, or off track? If at risk or off track, what specifically is blocking it and who is responsible for removing the block before the next review? The 10 minute review is not a status update meeting. It is an accountability mechanism. The difference is that status updates describe what has happened and accountability mechanisms ask what will be different before the next review. A management team that reviews initiative progress weekly in this format, consistently, in the same format, with the same three questions, catches problems while they are correctable and maintains the organizational visibility that transforms a strategic commitment into a strategic result.

Discipline 6 , Celebrating Completion, Not Launch

The most powerful cultural intervention available to a leadership team that wants to restore the organization's relationship with strategic execution is a simple change in what gets celebrated. Most mid-sized companies celebrate initiative launches. The new product announcement gets the all hands meeting. The new market entry gets the press release. The new operational improvement program gets the communication cascade. The actual completion of these initiatives, when it happens receives a fraction of the organizational recognition that the launch received. Shift the celebration from launch to completion. Make the delivery of a committed strategic result, on time, at the quality level committed, with the outcome promised, the organizational event that generates recognition, visibility, and reward. Within one planning cycle, this shift changes the management team's relationship with strategic commitments from performative to substantive.

What Focus Does for Morale

I want to address something that is often treated as a separate topic from strategic focus but that is, in my experience, its most direct and most immediate consequence: what happens to the organization's people when the number of simultaneous initiatives is reduced.

The organizational morale problem created by initiative overcommitment is not primarily a function of workload, though workload is a component of it. It is a function of futility. There is a specific quality of demoralization that comes from working hard on something that never gets finished, that never produces the result it was launched to achieve, and that is eventually superseded by a newer priority without the old one ever being formally completed or acknowledged. This is not burnout from effort. It is something closer to the corrosive hopelessness of effort that does not compound.

The most capable people in any organization have a specific relationship with meaningful work. They do not need to be protected from difficulty or shielded from demanding expectations. They need to believe that their effort is connected to an outcome that is real, that the organization behind them has made the commitments required to support their work, and that when they deliver, the delivery will be recognized as significant. Initiative overcommitment systematically destroys every one of these conditions.

What happens to the organization when focus is restored is not subtle. Within 60 to 90 days of implementing the three initiative portfolio, the behavioral signals that preceded the morale problem begin to reverse. The quality of contributions in management meetings improves, because the management team has a cleaner priority landscape to discuss. The pace of work on the retained initiatives accelerates, because the A players assigned to them no longer have competing claims on their attention. The organizational confidence that was eroded by a string of incomplete efforts begins to recover as the first completed initiative demonstrates that the organization is capable of finishing what it starts.

I have seen this recovery happen in companies of every size and sector, and it is consistently faster than leaders expect. The organizational capacity for productive work was not destroyed by the overcommitment, it was suppressed by it. Remove the suppression and the capacity returns, often with an energy that reflects the relief of working in an organization that knows what it is trying to accomplish and believes it can accomplish it.

> ***Your best people leave when they realize the company doesn't know what it's doing. Clarity retains them better than compensation ever will.***

The Underlying Principle: Ambition Requires Architecture

The ambition that drives mid-sized company growth is a genuine asset. I do not want anything in this article to be read as an argument against the confidence, the energy, or the expansive strategic thinking that characterize the best founder led organizations. Those qualities are not the problem. They are the fuel. The problem is the absence of organizational architecture that channels the fuel productively rather than allowing it to disperse.

The most ambitious organizations I have been part of or observed are not the ones that try to do the most things simultaneously. They are the ones that do fewer things with exceptional concentration.

The first success they achieve teaches them something important: that focused effort, sustained over time, produces results that dispersed effort never produces. The second success reinforces the lesson. By the third, the organizational culture of focused execution is embedded deeply enough that the management team begins to apply it instinctively, selecting fewer initiatives, resourcing them more completely, and holding the organization accountable to a standard of completion rather than launch.

This is the organization that sophisticated acquirors, investors, and banking partners recognize immediately when they encounter it. Not because it has done more than its competitors. Because what it has done, it has finished. Because the strategic commitments it has made, it has honored. Because the people who work in it look like people who work in an organization that knows what it is doing, which is to say they look engaged, confident, and proud of the work.

The three initiative rule is the operational expression of a principle that every founder and CEO who has ever been lost in an overcommitted portfolio already knows intuitively: you cannot do everything at once, and trying to is not ambition. It is the avoidance of the more difficult work of choosing.

Choosing is harder than adding. Subtracting is harder than growing. Finishing is harder than starting. These are the specific difficulties that separate the organizations that become genuinely great from the ones that become genuinely busy. The difference is not ambition. It is discipline. And discipline, applied to the question of organizational focus, is the highest leverage investment a mid-sized company CEO can make in the long term performance and the lasting health of the organization they are trying to build.

You cannot build a great organization by trying to do everything. You build one by doing a few things so well, with such consistency and

such concentration, that those things become the foundation everything else is built on.

Summary

The success trap described in this chapter is one of the most common strategic failure modes in a mid-sized company. A capable management team that has proven it can execute on multiple fronts takes on more than it can actually carry and ends up producing mediocre results across all of them instead of exceptional results on the few that matter most.

Management bandwidth does not expand simply because ambition does. The companies that move beyond this stage do not do so by building endless capacity for parallel execution. They do so by choosing fewer things and giving those things their best people, best attention, and best capital.

The three initiative rule is not a limit on ambition. It is the condition under which ambition becomes real. Before any initiative is authorized, however, there is a more basic decision test that most organizations still skip. The next chapter examines that test and the discipline of asking not only whether a plan is compelling, but how it is most likely to fail.

7

The Pre Mortem:The Decision Test Your Organization Is Not Running

THE QUESTION EVERY PLAN SKIPS: WHAT IF THIS FAILS?

The first time I ran a pre mortem on a major decision, I was not searching for a better planning tool. I was searching for an explanation.

The company had just completed a significant market expansion that consumed 18 months of management attention, a meaningful capital commitment, and the energy of some of our best people. At the time we approved it, the case looked sound. The market analysis was thorough. The financial projections were defensible. The team was experienced. The board approved it unanimously.

It failed. Not in a dramatic, company threatening way, but in a measurable and expensive one. The assumptions behind the expansion proved wrong in ways that looked painfully obvious once the result was visible. The competitive response in the target market was stronger than our analysis had acknowledged. Customer acquisition economics were worse than projected. The team leading the effort was stretched more thinly than anyone wanted to admit.

What stayed with me was not just that it failed. It was that, after it failed, every major cause seemed predictable. The competitive reaction we had minimized was a documented pattern in that type of market. The customer acquisition challenge was visible in the early pilot data. The management bandwidth risk had been raised by people whose concerns deserved more attention than they received.

The post mortem was honest and thorough. It also came a year too late.

That experience sent me looking for a different kind of test, one that could surface failure causes before the failure rather than after it. In the work of Gary Klein, the cognitive psychologist who studied expert decision making under uncertainty, I found a methodology so simple and so powerful that it has since become a non negotiable part of every consequential decision I participate in. Klein called it the pre mortem. I have often called it the practice I wish I had discovered twenty years earlier.

Post-mortems explain the failure. Pre-mortems prevent it.

What the Pre Mortem Is and Why It Works

Gary Klein's insight emerged from research on how expert teams make decisions in high stakes environments, including military units, firefighters, and clinical teams. What he observed was that most planning processes are built to improve and support a plan. They are not built to surface the specific ways a plan is likely to fail.

The pre mortem flips that orientation. Instead of asking how do we make this succeed, it asks a more unsettling question: imagine it is twelve months from now and this decision has failed badly. Not stumbled, failed. What happened?

The power of the method lies in the instruction to assume failure rather than merely consider it. When a team is asked what could go wrong, the group's normal social pressures begin working immediately. People do not want to sound disloyal. They do not want to derail a plan the group has already invested in. They do not want to raise a concern that might later prove unfounded.

When the same group is told this has already failed, explain why, the psychology changes. The team is no longer being asked to criticize the plan. It is being asked to explain an assumed outcome. That shift frees people to identify risks they were already seeing but were reluctant to voice.

Prospective hindsight, the cognitive act of reasoning backward from an assumed outcome, reliably surfaces more failure causes than forward looking analysis alone. In a mid-sized company, where one major decision can absorb the better part of a year's management attention and a meaningful portion of the company's capital, that difference is not academic. It materially improves decision quality.

The post-mortem is the most honest conversation in the building. The pre-mortem is that honesty, moved to when it still matters.

Why Most Planning Processes Avoid the Question

The pre mortem is simple. That is not the same thing as easy. Most planning processes are structured around commitment. A strategy is developed. A plan is refined. A board approves it. A communication cascade announces it. At each step, the social and professional momentum behind the plan grows.

By the time a strategic initiative is formally approved, the people in the room have usually invested weeks or months in building, defending, and aligning around it. Raising a fundamental concern at that stage carries a real psychological cost. No one wants to be seen as obstructive. No one wants to challenge a colleague who has worked hard on the proposal. No one wants to be the person who introduces doubt after the group has already begun signaling commitment.

The result is that the concerns most important to decision quality are often the ones least likely to be voiced in the formal planning process. They exist in the room. They just do not surface in the room.

Over the years I learned to recognize the signals that a team had concerns it was not saying aloud. A pause before agreement. A private comment after the meeting. A cautious phrase in a hallway conversation that never appeared in the official discussion. Those signals were present in the expansion effort that failed. What was missing was a process that made those concerns legitimate to raise before the decision became final.

The pre mortem creates that process. It gives people a role and a script for surfacing what they already suspect. Identifying a failure cause is not disloyalty in a pre mortem. It is the assignment.

The pre-mortem takes the concerns no one dared to voice and makes them mandatory.

What the Process Consistently Surfaces

Once I began running pre mortems systematically, a pattern emerged. Across strategic plans, capital investments, major hires, acquisitions, and market launches, the exercise repeatedly surfaced the same three categories of failure cause that the preceding planning process had missed or minimized.

First, it surfaces underestimated competitive response. Plans involving market action almost always assume a slower or weaker competitor reaction than reality produces. Teams know their own capabilities more intimately than they know their competitors, and that imbalance quietly biases the analysis.

Second, it surfaces execution dependency fragility. Most plans assume a level of organizational capacity and coordination that looks plausible on paper and proves more fragile in practice. The pre mortem flushes out the key person risk, the cross functional handoff risk, and the management bandwidth risk that formal planning tends to underweight.

Third, and most valuably, it surfaces assumption fragility. Every significant plan rests on a small number of assumptions that are both likely to be wrong and highly consequential if they are wrong. The best pre mortem sessions identify those assumptions clearly enough that the team can go back and test them with the rigor they should have received in the first place.

In practice, that is often the highest value outcome of the exercise. The pre mortem does not merely make the team more cautious. It makes the team more specific about what must be true for the decision to work.

Five Decision Categories That Require a Pre Mortem

Strategic plans and annual operating plans

A strategic plan directs the company's resources for the next year or longer. It is also the decision with the most organizational momentum behind it by the time it reaches final approval. The pre mortem should force the team to ask: if this plan has failed by year end, what market assumption proved wrong, what capability we assumed we had turned out to be unavailable, and what competitive development we discounted proved decisive?

Capital investments above a defined threshold

Any significant capital request should be stress tested before money is committed. The critical question is straightforward: if this investment produces less than half its projected return, what caused the shortfall? In my experience the answers usually cluster around revenue assumptions that were too optimistic, implementation timelines that were too short, and costs that were not fully accounted for.

Senior hires at the director level and above

A failed senior hire is costly in more ways than one. It absorbs time, delays capability building, disrupts teams, and sends cultural signals throughout the organization. The pre mortem question here is: if this person is no longer in this role eighteen months from now, what happened? That framing often surfaces expectation mismatches, style conflicts, and contextual issues that did not show up in the interview process.

Market entries and product initiatives

New markets and new products carry high variance and high optimism. Teams are often more familiar with the existing business than with the buying behavior they are trying to project. The right question is: if this initiative has failed to gain meaningful traction in twelve months, what happened? That usually leads to a more honest conversation about customer demand, competitive alternatives, sales model fit, and runway.

Acquisitions and significant partnerships

These are the highest stakes decisions available to most mid-sized companies. If the transaction has failed to generate its thesis return in three years, what happened? The most common answers involve integration burden, faster than expected talent loss, and synergies that proved smaller, slower, or more conditional than assumed.

The Six Step Pre Mortem Protocol

Step 1: Assume the failure

Open the session with a blunt instruction: it is twelve months from today and this decision has failed badly. Not stumbled, failed in a way that is materially damaging to the company. Your job is not to prevent the failure. It has already happened. Your job is to explain it. The past tense matters. The moment the room returns to talking about whether failure might occur, forward optimism reenters the conversation.

Step 2: Silent write before discussion

Give every participant five to seven minutes to write their failure causes individually and in silence. This step is essential. Once group discussion begins, the room starts anchoring to the first concerns raised and to the most senior voices present. Silent individual analysis protects the range and honesty of the initial assessment.

Step 3: Structured round robin collection

Collect failure causes one at a time from each participant until the list is exhausted. Record every cause without debate. During this phase the goal is data gathering, not evaluation. The moment someone starts arguing with a cause, other people start censoring themselves.

Step 4: Prioritize by probability and consequence

Once the list is complete, evaluate each item on two dimensions: how likely it is to occur given the current plan and environment, and how severe its consequences would be if it did occur. The items that rank high on both dimensions are the pre mortem's most important output.

Step 5: Decide how the plan will respond

For each high priority risk, the team should choose one of three responses. Strengthen the plan so the failure becomes less likely or less damaging. Mitigate the risk by identifying a contingency response if warning signs emerge. Or reconsider the decision if the risk is both highly probable and potentially fatal and cannot be responsibly reduced.

Step 6: Record kill criteria and monitoring signals

The exercise becomes operational only when it ends in written management rules. For each material failure cause that remains, define the kill criterion, the condition under which the plan will be paused or stopped, and the monitoring signal, the leading indicator that shows the risk is approaching. Those two elements turn the pre mortem from an interesting discussion into a management tool.

The Culture Requirement

The pre mortem does not work in a culture that punishes the honest identification of failure causes. I have seen sessions collapse into superficiality because a CEO signaled impatience with the concerns being raised. A slight posture change, a dismissive phrase, or a quick rebuttal is enough to tell the room which risks are safe to discuss and which are not.

When that happens, the session still produces a list. It just produces the wrong list. The risks that matter most remain unspoken, and the pre mortem becomes a procedural box check rather than a meaningful stress test.

For the method to work, leadership has to establish two conditions. First, identifying a failure cause can never be treated as disloyalty to the plan or its sponsors. Second, the person who surfaces the risk that later proves most consequential must be recognized, not penalized.

In the companies I have run, I often facilitated the most important pre mortems myself, not as the plan's advocate but as the room's collector of failure modes. That role sends a clear signal. The purpose of the session is not to defend the proposal. It is to learn from the scenario in which it has failed.

The pre-mortem takes an hour. The honesty it requires takes years — and starts with the CEO.

Make It a Governance Requirement

The final point is the one I feel most strongly about. The pre mortem should not be an optional best practice that leaders apply when they remember to or when a decision feels unusually uncertain. It should be a governance requirement.

The decisions that most need a pre mortem are often the ones that feel most certain, because certainty is exactly the condition in which optimism bias is most powerful and honest dissent is least likely to surface on its own.

For a mid-sized company, the governance architecture is straightforward. Define the categories and thresholds that require a pre mortem as a condition of authorization. Document the high priority failure causes, the planned responses, the kill criteria, and the monitoring signals. Include that record in the materials presented to the CEO or the board for approval.

This does not add significant friction. A rigorous pre mortem takes sixty to ninety minutes. The written summary takes a little longer. For a decision that will consume months of management attention and a meaningful amount of capital, that is not delay. It is one of the highest leverage uses of management time available.

I think of it as the managerial equivalent of an engineering stress test. You do not test a bridge because you expect it to fail. You test it because the consequences of an untested failure are worse than the cost of the test. Significant decisions deserve the same discipline.

The post mortem is honest. It is also too late. The pre mortem is honest at the only moment when honesty can still improve the result: before the decision is made, while the outcome is still open, and while the company still has all of its options available.

Planning is built to avoid one question: what if this fails? The pre-mortem makes that question the starting point.

Summary

What Gary Klein identified in the pre mortem, and what this chapter translates into the practical life of a mid-sized company, is a simple truth that feels uncomfortable precisely because it is so useful. The people in the room usually already know most of the ways the plan could fail. They simply do not say so because the social and professional dynamics of planning suppress that honesty in favor of visible commitment.

The pre mortem does not give the organization new analytical ability. It gives the organization permission to apply the intelligence it already has. A plan that has survived a serious pre mortem has earned its authorization in a way most plans never do. But authorization is still not execution. The next problem begins once the plan leaves the leadership room and meets the front line, where the gap between what leadership intended and what people actually do becomes the real determinant of results.

8

Why Your Strategy Looks Different on the Front Line Than It Does in the Boardroom

STRATEGY DIES IN THE GAP BETWEEN "WE TOLD THEM" AND "THEY UNDERSTOOD", AND THAT GAP IS FIXABLE.

I have conducted a specific test at the beginning of every new engagement with a mid-sized company management team, and the results have been consistent enough over the years that I have stopped expecting them to vary.

I ask each member of the senior leadership team, individually, before any group conversation, to answer one question: what are the three most important things the company must accomplish in the next twelve months for the business to be materially stronger than it is today?

The answers are almost never the same from person to person. Not slightly different, fundamentally different. Different priorities, different timeframes, different underlying assumptions about what the company's most pressing challenge is. The Chief Revenue Officer describes a customer acquisition imperative. The Chief Operating

Officer describes an efficiency transformation. The CFO describes a working capital problem. The CEO, when asked last, describes a strategic initiative that was presented to the board three months earlier and that the other members of the leadership team have not referenced at all.

This is a management team that has been working together for years. They have sat through the same planning retreats, received the same strategy documents, and attended the same all hands meetings. They have, by any reasonable organizational definition, been communicated to. And yet they cannot agree on the company's three most important priorities.

If the senior leadership team cannot agree on the strategy in a private conversation with an outside advisor, what is happening to the strategy four levels down in the organization, at the front line where the daily decisions that determine whether the strategy succeeds or fails are made? I have asked this question directly of frontline employees in companies I have run and companies I have advised. The answers are illuminating and humbling. Most frontline employees can describe what they do every day with precision and energy. Very few can describe how what they do every day connects to where the company is trying to go.

Kaplan and Norton, in their research on strategy execution failure, found that fewer than five percent of frontline employees could name their organization's top five strategic priorities. I have not found reason to doubt that finding. I have found ample reason to believe the problem is worse in mid-sized companies, where the formal communication infrastructure of a large corporation, the internal communications function, the cascade processes, the manager training programs, does not exist, and where the CEO's direct communication reach ends somewhere around the director level.

Strategy doesn't fail in communication. It fails in translation.

The Distinction That Changes Everything: Communication Versus Translation

Before describing what goes wrong and what fixes it, I want to establish a distinction that I believe is the conceptual key to this entire problem. Most organizations treat the strategy communication challenge as a volume and format problem: the strategy needs to be communicated more frequently, in more formats, through more channels. More all hands meetings. More written summaries. More manager cascade sessions. More visual strategy posters in the hallway.

This approach fails consistently, and it fails for a specific reason: it assumes that what frontline employees are missing is information about the strategy. In my experience, that is almost never the problem. The problem is not that frontline employees lack information about the strategy. It is that they cannot use the information they have.

A strategy expressed in the language of senior management, competitive positioning, revenue mix optimization, operational leverage, customer lifetime value, is information. It is accurate, important, and entirely inaccessible to a warehouse supervisor, a field service technician, or an inside sales representative making twenty decisions a day about how to allocate their time and energy. Those decisions are not made against a strategic framework. They are made against habit, immediate feedback, and whatever the last manager who walked past the desk seemed to care about.

Translation is different from communication. Communication moves information from one place to another. Translation converts information from one form into another, specifically, from the form that is meaningful to the person who produced it into the form that is meaningful to the person who needs to act on it. The strategy that is meaningful to a CEO is expressed in financial and competitive terms. The strategy that is meaningful to a frontline employee is expressed in behavioral terms: what should I do differently on Tuesday than I did last Tuesday? What decision should I make differently when I face the choice I face every week? Which customer request should I prioritize and which should I deprioritize, and why?

Until the strategy has been converted from financial and competitive language into specific behavioral language that every member of the organization can apply in the course of their daily work, it has not been communicated. It has been announced.

A strategy hasn't been communicated until people can tell you what they'll do differently tomorrow.

The Five Gaps Between the Boardroom and the Front Line

The distance between the strategy as conceived in the boardroom and the strategy as understood on the front line is not a single gap. It is a series of gaps, each introduced at a different stage of the communication process, each compounding the distortion introduced by the previous one. Understanding where the gaps originate is the prerequisite for knowing where to intervene.

Gap 1. The Abstraction Gap

What management believes has been communicated. The strategy has been clearly articulated in financial and competitive terms. Management believes the logic is straightforward: grow revenue in our highest margin segments while reducing operational costs in our lower efficiency processes. The direction is clear.

What the front line actually received. The front line receives an aspiration with no operational definition. Grow what? Which segments exactly? How do I know when a customer belongs to a high margin segment? Reduce costs how? What does 'lower efficiency' mean in the context of what I do today? The strategy describes a destination in terms that are entirely meaningful to the person who designed it and entirely meaningless to the person who must navigate toward it.

Gap 2. The Cascade Dilution Gap

What management believes has been communicated. The strategy was communicated to the senior leadership team with full context, analytical grounding, and the competitive rationale that makes the direction compelling. Management is confident that the leadership team will cascade it effectively to their direct reports.

What the front line actually received. Each management layer in the cascade translates the strategy into the terms most relevant to its own functional reality, stripping away the strategic context that makes the direction coherent. By the time the strategy reaches the front line through three or four management layers, it has been converted into a series of functional directives, metrics targets, process changes, new reporting requirements, that have no visible connection to the strategic logic that generated them. The front line is executing someone's interpretation of someone's interpretation of the strategy.

Gap 3. The Priority Conflict Gap

What management believes has been communicated. The strategy has been announced with appropriate emphasis on its importance. Management believes the organization understands that the strategic priorities are the most important things to be working on.

What the front line actually received. The front line receives the strategic priorities alongside every existing operational requirement, every existing performance metric, and every existing accountability structure, none of which have been changed to reflect the new strategic direction. The new priorities compete on equal terms with the old ones and lose, because the old ones are embedded in the management system that determines what gets measured, what gets recognized, and what determines whether a front line employee's performance is judged as good or poor.

Gap 4. The Vocabulary Gap

What management believes has been communicated. The strategy document uses the vocabulary of management: strategic priority, competitive differentiation, operational excellence, customer centric approach, value creation. Management considers this vocabulary precise and meaningful.

What the front line actually received. The front line hears language that sounds important but carries no operational content. 'Customer centric' does not tell a customer service representative which of two competing customer needs to prioritize when they conflict. 'Operational excellence' does not tell a production supervisor which process to change first. 'Strategic priority' does not tell a salesperson which customer segment to spend Tuesday afternoon calling. Management vocabulary communicates aspiration. Behavioral vocabulary communicates instruction.

Gap 5. The Feedback Silence Gap

What management believes has been communicated. The strategy has been communicated and management is monitoring the metrics that indicate whether execution is on track. The communication process is considered complete.

What the front line actually received. The front line has no mechanism for communicating back to management the specific ways in which the strategy does not match operational reality, the customer behavior that contradicts the strategic assumption, the competitive dynamic in the field that differs from the competitive analysis in the boardroom, the process requirement that makes the strategic directive impractical as written. The strategy travels in one direction. The intelligence that would improve it is trapped at the front line with no path to the people who could act on it.

What the Gap Looks Like in Practice

I want to describe a specific pattern I have encountered enough times to consider it representative. The details change, the sector, the revenue level, the specific strategy being implemented, but the underlying dynamic is the same.

A mid-sized company has spent the better part of a quarter developing a market focus strategy. The company has historically served all comers across a broad range of customer types and transaction sizes. The new strategy calls for a deliberate shift of sales and service resources toward a specific customer profile: larger accounts in two or three target verticals with demonstrably higher lifetime value and lower service complexity. The financial logic is sound. The management team is aligned. The board has approved it.

The strategy is announced at an all hands meeting. The CEO presents the competitive rationale, the financial projections, and the organizational implications. The strategy document is distributed. The management team holds cascade sessions with their direct reports. The strategy is on the website, in the quarterly communication to employees, and on the poster in the break room that nobody reads after the first week.

Six months later, the sales team is still spending the majority of its time on small, high complexity accounts. Not because they are opposed to the strategy. Not because they have not heard about it. Because the CRM system still measures total deals closed, not deals closed in target verticals. Because the commission structure still pays the same rate on all revenue. Because the sales manager's performance review still references total pipeline value. Because the last three times a salesperson prioritized a smaller deal in a target vertical over a larger deal outside it, nobody noticed the strategic alignment and everybody noticed the revenue shortfall.

The strategy has been communicated. It has not been translated into the management system that determines behavior. And behavior, not communication, not aspiration, not the poster in the break room, is what strategy execution actually is.

Strategy isn't executed by the people who wrote it. It's executed — or undermined — in thousands of daily decisions by people who never read it.

The Three Translation Questions That Close the Gap

The translation approach I have developed and refined through direct application in companies I have run and advised begins with three questions that must be answered for every strategic priority before it is considered genuinely communicated. These questions are the bridge between strategic language and behavioral language. They convert the strategy from a description of where the company is trying to go into a set of specific decisions the front line can use to navigate there.

The questions are deceptively simple. They are also rarely asked, because most strategy communication processes end at the announcement and never reach the translation.

The Three Translation Questions

Question 1. If a frontline employee in [specific role] had to make a different decision tomorrow because of this strategy, what specific decision would it be? Describe the specific situation in which that decision arises, the choice between two concrete options, and the specific option the strategy points toward.

Question 2. If a frontline employee in [specific role] did exactly the right thing for this strategy in a given week, what would we see them doing or not doing? Describe the specific observable behavior, not the attitude, not the commitment, not the understanding, the specific action or inaction that would tell us the strategy is working at the execution level.

Question 3. If a frontline employee in [specific role] did exactly the wrong thing for this strategy, not because they were lazy or disengaged, but because the existing management system is pointing them in the wrong direction, what specific behavior would we see? What does the current incentive, metric, or management signal tell them to do that conflicts with what the strategy requires?

These three questions, applied rigorously to every strategic priority for every role in the organization, produce something that a strategy document and a cascade presentation do not produce: a specific, behavioral description of what the strategy means at every level of the organization.

They also produce something else that is equally valuable: an immediate inventory of the management system conflicts that are preventing the strategy from reaching the front line. The answer to the third question, what is the legacy management system telling people to do that conflicts with the strategy, is almost always longer and more specific than the management team expects. It describes the specific metrics, incentives, approval processes, and manager behaviors that are actively competing with the strategy for the front line's attention and winning.

I have facilitated this translation exercise in enough organizations to say with confidence that the answers to these three questions, assembled for every role and every strategic priority, produce a more accurate picture of the strategy's execution prospects than any financial model or risk assessment the organization has conducted. The financial model describes what happens if the strategy works as planned. The translation exercise describes whether the strategy has any meaningful chance of working at all.

Six Practices That Make Strategy Executable at Every Level

The translation questions identify the problem and the required content. The following six practices are the organizational mechanisms through which that content reaches the front line and stays there. They are not communication programs. They are management system changes, adjustments to the organizational infrastructure that determines what behavior is measured, rewarded, and reinforced at every level.

Practice 1. The Strategy On One Page, In Plain Language

Every strategic priority must be expressible in one sentence that contains no management vocabulary and that a front line employee in any function can read and immediately understand the behavioral implication. Not 'achieve operational excellence through continuous improvement' but 'complete every customer order within 24 hours of confirmation, and when you cannot, call the customer before they call us.' Not 'grow revenue in high value customer segments' but 'spend 60 percent of your customer facing time this quarter with companies that have more than 50 employees in our target industries.' The test for whether a strategic priority has been expressed in plain language is simple: give the one sentence description to a frontline employee you have not previously spoken with about the strategy and ask them to describe in their own words what it means for their work tomorrow. If they can do it accurately, the translation is complete. If they cannot, the communication is not finished.

Practice 2. Align The Measurement System To The Strategy Before Announcing It

The single most effective change a CEO can make to improve strategy execution at the front line costs nothing and requires no new communication infrastructure: change what gets measured before the strategy is announced rather than after the strategy has failed to change behavior. If the strategy calls for focus on high value customer segments, the measurement system must capture performance in those segments specifically, before the salesforce is told to focus on them. If the strategy calls for service quality improvement, the measurement system must capture the specific service quality indicators the strategy targets, before the service team is told to improve them. A strategy that is announced before the measurement system reflects it is a strategy that will produce the same behavior as before, reported against different language. When measurement and strategy are aligned from day one, the front line receives a consistent signal rather than a mixed one.

Practice 3. Rewrite The Incentives To Reflect Strategic Priorities

Compensation and recognition systems are the most powerful behavioral direction mechanisms available to a CEO, and the ones most consistently misaligned with strategic priorities in mid-sized companies. The typical pattern: a new strategy is announced that calls for a behavioral shift, from volume to margin, from new customer acquisition to existing customer retention, from broad market coverage to focused vertical penetration, but the incentive structure continues to reward the behaviors of the prior strategy. The front line correctly identifies the real priority as the one that determines their compensation and acts accordingly. Adjusting the incentive structure to reflect strategic priorities, even modestly, adding a 20 or 30 percent weight to the new strategic behavior alongside the existing volume based incentives, produces behavioral change faster than any communication program. It also sends a specific organizational signal: this strategy is real, not aspirational, because the company has put money behind it.

Practice 4. Give Every Manager A Conversation Guide, Not A Slide Deck

The cascade through management layers is where more strategic intent is lost than in any other part of the communication process. The reason is not that managers are poor communicators. It is that managers are given presentation materials, slide decks, summary documents, FAQ sheets, that are designed to convey information, not to facilitate the specific behavioral translation conversations that turn strategic information into strategic understanding. Replace the slide deck with a conversation guide. The conversation guide is a single page that gives every manager three things: the one sentence behavioral description of each strategic priority for the roles they manage; three specific questions to ask each direct report to assess whether the translation has been understood; and three specific situations in which the manager should reference the strategic priority in the course of their weekly interactions with the team. The conversation guide does not produce understanding through presentation. It produces understanding through repeated, specific, contextual dialogue.

Practice 5. Create A Mechanism For Front Line Intelligence To Reach Leadership

The fifth gap, the feedback silence, is the one that compounds all the others over time. A strategy that is not revised based on front line intelligence about the gap between strategic assumptions and operational reality will drift further from executable as time passes. The mechanism does not need to be sophisticated. It needs to be real: a specific channel through which frontline employees can surface strategic conflicts, the customer behavior that contradicts the strategic assumption, the competitive reality in the field that differs from the boardroom analysis, without the information being filtered or suppressed by the management layers it must pass through to reach the CEO. The most reliable mechanisms I have seen are simple: a monthly thirty minute CEO roundtable with a rotating group of front line employees; a weekly written question from the CEO to the front line, answered anonymously and summarized for leadership; or a standing agenda item in the weekly operations meeting specifically for front line intelligence that challenges a strategic assumption.

Practice 6. Replace The Annual Communication Event With A Weekly Strategic Reference

The most enduring failure in strategy communication is the organizational calendar: the strategy is communicated intensively at the annual planning cycle and then referenced only when quarterly results fall short of projections. In between, the operational calendar, the weekly management meeting, the monthly performance review, the daily operational decisions, contains almost no reference to the strategy. The strategy recedes from organizational consciousness not through disagreement or resistance but through the entirely predictable process of attention displacement. The fix is structural: make the strategy a standing element of every weekly management meeting, every monthly performance conversation, and every significant operational decision. Not a lengthy strategic review, a brief, consistent, specific reference. When a significant decision is being made, the question 'how does this advance our three strategic priorities?' should be as automatic as the question 'what does this cost?' That consistency, not the intensity of the initial communication event, is what embeds the strategy in organizational behavior.

What Changes When Translation Is Taken Seriously

I want to describe what the organization actually looks and feels like when the strategy to execution translation has been done well, because the description of the problem and its solutions can obscure what is, in my experience, the most immediately observable indicator of translation success: the quality of the conversations that happen at every level of the organization.

In an organization where the translation gap is large, where the strategy exists in the boardroom but not at the front line, the conversations that happen at the management meeting and the conversations that happen on the front line are about different things. Management is discussing strategic priorities, competitive positioning, and progress against the plan. The front line is discussing customer demands, operational problems, and the daily challenges of doing the job. There is no conversation that connects the two. The strategy and the operations are running as parallel systems with no meaningful intersection.

In an organization where the translation has been completed, where every front line employee can describe how their daily decisions connect to the company's strategic direction, the conversations are different at every level. The front line employee who declines a small transaction outside the target segment because it conflicts with where the company is focusing is not following a rule. he is making a strategic judgment that he has internalized because the strategy was translated into terms he could apply. The sales manager who coaches a rep on vertical focus rather than volume is not complying with a directive. He is reinforcing a strategic priority that his own understanding of the strategy made concrete.

These are not heroic moments of organizational alignment. They are the cumulative effect of thousands of ordinary decisions made by people who understand not just what the company is trying to do, but specifically what they should do differently as a result. That specific, behavioral, actionable understanding, not the strategic plan, not the communication cascade, not the all hands meeting, is what strategy execution actually is.

And it requires, above all, one organizational commitment: the willingness of leadership to do the harder, slower, less visible work of translation rather than the easier, faster, more impressive work of announcement. Announcement is an event. Translation is a discipline. The organizations that consistently execute their strategies are the ones that have chosen discipline over event, and that have built the management systems to sustain it.

When a frontline employee can explain the strategy in her own words, that isn't communication. That's translation — and it doesn't happen by accident.

Leadership Responsibility That Cannot Be Delegated

I want to close with something that I have learned from running companies and from watching other executives run theirs: the strategy to front line translation is the CEO's responsibility in a way that no other communication task is.

It is tempting to delegate this work. The internal communications team produces the strategy document. The HR team designs the cascade process. The training team develops the manager communication guides. Each of these functions can contribute to the translation effort and should. But the translation cannot be completed by any of them, because the translation requires something that only the CEO and the senior leadership team possess: the ability to answer the question 'why does this strategy matter' with the specific, personal conviction that comes from having built the competitive analysis, wrestled with the trade offs, and committed to the direction.

A strategy communicated by a communications team is a corporate message. A strategy communicated by the CEO, in specific terms, in multiple formats, in repeated genuine conversations that demonstrate personal engagement with the translation challenge, is an organizational belief. The difference between a corporate message and an organizational belief is the difference between a strategy that is known and a strategy that is acted on.

In the companies I have run, the moments of greatest strategic clarity, the moments when I could walk the floor and find frontline employees making decisions that reflected the strategy without being asked, without being monitored, without knowing I was watching, were always the product of sustained, personal, specific communication from the top. Not the all hands meeting. Not the strategy poster. The repeated, specific, sometimes tedious work of sitting with small groups, asking the translation questions, listening to the answers, correcting the misunderstandings, and doing it again the following week.

That work is not glamorous. It does not appear in the business press coverage of strategic leadership. It does not generate the kind of organizational enthusiasm that a bold strategic announcement produces. But it is the work that determines whether the bold strategic announcement becomes organizational reality or organizational aspiration. And in my experience, it is the most important work a CEO does.

Strategy execution isn't measured in planning cycles. It's measured in conversations.

Summary

The central distinction in this chapter is the one most strategy execution writing passes over too quickly. Communication moves strategy from one place to another. Translation converts it into the behavioral language that tells a frontline employee what to do differently tomorrow than they did yesterday.

The five gaps described here are not unusual errors in process design. They are the predictable consequence of treating strategy communication as a volume problem rather than a translation problem. The organizations that close these gaps do not simply communicate more often. They convert strategy into specific behavioral direction, align the measurement system to the new priorities, and build the upward feedback loops that allow frontline experience to reach the people who can act on it.

With operations and strategy now in view, the book turns to the commercial engine underneath both, what the company sells, how it sells it, and what that commercial activity actually turns into in cash.

9

How You Sell Changes Everything: The Marketing and Sales Evolution Every Mid-Size Company Must Navigate

Services, Products, Technology: Three Different Sales Games That Most Founders Learn the Hard Way. Here's the Map.

I have built and led companies that sold professional services, companies that sold manufactured products, and companies that sold technology platforms. I have advised founders across all three categories as they tried to grow past the early stage and into the mid-sized range where the real organizational complexity begins.

The single observation I would offer to any founder who has succeeded in one of these categories and is tempted to assume the lessons are transferable is this: they are not. Not in the way that matters most. The strategies, the people, the sales cycles, the marketing architectures, and the owner's role in the revenue process are so specifically different across services, products, and technology that companies which attempt to apply the go-to-market model of one category to another consistently produce expensive and time-consuming failures.

But there is something equally important, and equally misunderstood, about the evolution that occurs within any single category as a mid-sized company grows from 15 million to 75 million dollars in revenue. The selling model that produced the first growth phase is almost never the right model for the next. The salesperson who excels at the early stage is rarely the one who excels at scale. The level of owner involvement that was necessary and productive at 20 million dollars in revenue becomes an organizational ceiling at 50 million dollars. The informal word-of-mouth pipeline that funded the company's founding growth is insufficient to fund its scaling growth.

Most founders learn these things the hard way: by hiring the wrong people, waiting too long for pipelines to develop, staying personally involved in deals long after their involvement stops adding value, and watching the company stall at a revenue threshold that was not a market limit but a go-to-market design limit.

This article is the map I wish more founders had earlier. It addresses both dimensions of the marketing and sales evolution challenge: the fundamental differences across selling models depending on what you sell, and the specific transformations that every mid-sized company must navigate as it grows regardless of what it sells.

How you sell isn't tactics. It's the business model. Misunderstand it, and you'll underperform the opportunity your product deserves.

The Three Fundamentally Different Selling Models

Before any discussion of how the selling function evolves as a company grows, it is necessary to be precise about the fundamental differences between the three primary selling models available to mid-sized companies. The differences are not superficial. They determine who you hire, how you structure the revenue generation process, what marketing activities produce returns, and how involved the owner or CEO must be in the commercial function.

Model 1: Selling Professional Services

The salesperson profile: The professional services salesperson is not primarily a sales professional. he is a domain expert who sells. The most effective sellers of services are people who understand the problem being solved at the same depth as the client experiencing it, which means the most effective sellers are often former practitioners of the service, not trained salespeople. A management consulting firm sells through consultants, not through a sales organization. An engineering services firm sells through engineers, not through a business development team. The credibility that closes a professional services relationship is the credibility of the person who will deliver the work, not the credibility of a separate sales function.

The sales cycle reality: The professional services sales cycle is long, relationship-dependent, and non-linear. A typical enterprise services engagement takes six to 18 months from first contact to signed contract because the buyer is making a decision about trusting a team with a significant organizational challenge. There is rarely a moment when the prospect decides to buy. There is a slow accumulation of confidence in the capability and judgment of the people they are evaluating. The sales process is not a funnel. It is a relationship investment whose return accrues unpredictably over a period that cannot be managed to a quota cycle, but managed with respect to its unpredictability.

The owner's role: In professional services, the owner is the primary selling asset in the early years and must remain deeply involved in the most significant relationships at every stage. This is not a design flaw, it is a feature of the selling model. The CEO's personal credibility, network, and domain reputation are the primary marketing assets of a professional services firm below 50 million dollars in revenue. The transition away from personal selling by the owner is the most difficult go-to-market evolution in professional services and the one that most consistently determines whether the firm scales beyond the founder's personal bandwidth.

Model 2: Selling Products

The salesperson profile: The product salesperson is a commercial professional whose job is to match a defined, documented offering to a qualified buyer's articulated need. Unlike the services seller, the product salesperson does not need deep technical expertise in the product's engineering or design, he needs deep knowledge of the customer's buying process, competitive landscape, and the specific value proposition that differentiates the product in the market. The best product salespeople are often the best closers: people who can navigate the commercial process efficiently, manage the objection cycle, and bring the decision to conclusion.

The sales cycle reality: Product sales cycles are more predictable and more amenable to pipeline management than professional services cycles, but they vary enormously based on the price point and organizational complexity of the purchase. A t 20 thousand-dollar product sold to a mid-sized company operations manager has a 30 to 60 day sales cycle. A 500 thousand-dollar capital equipment purchase requiring board approval has a 12 to 18 month cycle with a six-month evaluation process. The predictability of the product sales cycle is one of the primary commercial advantages of the product model over the services model, but only if the company has built the pipeline management discipline to exploit it.

The owner's role: The owner's role in product selling evolves most rapidly and most naturally of the three models. In the early stage, the founder is the company's best salesperson because he embodies the product's origin story and competitive differentiation. As the company builds a sales team with genuine product knowledge and customer relationship capability, the founder's involvement should transition from deal management to relationship escalation: he is the executive resource for the largest strategic accounts and the relationships where his personal authority adds commercial value, not the daily manager of the pipeline.

Model 3: Selling Technology

The salesperson profile: The technology salesperson operates in a selling environment that combines the domain credibility requirements of professional services with the pipeline management requirements of product selling, and adds the unique challenge of selling something the buyer cannot fully evaluate until they have experienced it. The most effective technology sellers are people who can simultaneously navigate a technical evaluation, a commercial negotiation, a competitive displacement, and an internal change management process on the buyer's side. This is a rare and expensive combination of capabilities, and mid-sized technology companies consistently underpay for it, overhire from the wrong talent pools, and underinvest in the enablement that makes good technology sellers exceptional.

The sales cycle reality: Technology sales cycles are driven by two factors that the services and product models manage differently:

the buyer's internal change management requirement and the competitive evaluation process. Technology purchases require the buyer to change how they work, which means the selling process must address not just the technical and commercial decision but the organizational adoption decision. This adds complexity to the cycle and introduces stakeholders who are not present in most product or services selling processes. A typical enterprise technology sale above 100 thousand dollars in annual contract value involves three to seven internal decision-makers at the buyer, each with different evaluation criteria, and a competitive process against two to four alternative solutions.

The owner's role: In technology selling, the CEO's involvement in the largest deals is a structural requirement throughout the scaling phase, not because the salesforce lacks capability, but because technology purchase decisions at significant contract values are relationship decisions as much as product decisions, and the CEO's personal engagement signals a level of vendor commitment that middle-market buyers require before they are willing to take the organizational risk of a technology change. The CEO who withdraws from the revenue process in technology selling before the company has built a genuine enterprise sales capability will watch its largest deal win rates decline.

Where Every Company Starts: The Combined Role Problem

Every mid-sized company, regardless of what it sells, begins its commercial life in the same organizational state: the same people who sell the product or service also deliver it, and the same people who deliver it also service it. The founder who closes the deal is often the founder who does the work. The account manager who manages the relationship is the project manager who runs the engagement. The person who delivers the product also handles the complaints when the product does not perform as expected.

This combined role model is not a design failure. It is the only sensible organizational structure for a company with limited headcount, limited capital, and the need for every person to be maximally productive in a resource-constrained environment. A team of eight cannot support dedicated sales, dedicated delivery, and dedicated customer service functions. The blended role is the rational response to organizational reality.

The problem is not that the combined role model exists. The problem is that it persists long past the point at which the company's growth requires it to evolve. I have observed this in companies across all three selling models, and the persistence mechanism is the same in every case: the combined role model works well enough in the short term that no single quarter produces an obvious crisis, even as the compounding cost of maintaining it erodes performance across all three functions simultaneously.

The salesperson who is also responsible for delivery has an inherent conflict of interest in the sales process: he is incentivized to undersell the implementation complexity and the delivery timeline because he is the one who will have to deliver. The delivery professional who is also responsible for customer service has an inherent conflict of interest in the service process: he is incentivized to resolve customer complaints in ways that minimize disruption to her delivery schedule rather than in ways that optimize the customer experience. The founder who is responsible for all three is the most constrained person in the organization because the combined role pulls his attention simultaneously in three directions that require fundamentally different modes of engagement.

Every mid-sized company outgrows the combined sell-deliver-service role. Most just don't outgrow it fast enough.

The Four Stages of Commercial Evolution in a Mid-Sized Company

The evolution from combined selling-delivery-service to a mature, separated commercial function is not a single transition. It is a sequence of four distinct stages, each with its own organizational structure, its own tension, and its own specific failure mode that must be managed if the company is to move successfully to the next stage.

Stage 1: $0 To $10 Million: The Founder-Led Commercial Engine

How selling, delivery, and service operate: Everything commercial is done by the founder and a small core team. The founder sells, delivers, and services the first customers personally. Every significant commercial relationship is a relationship with the founder. The pipeline is entirely referral-driven: every new customer is either a direct contact of the founder or a referral from an existing customer who is a direct contact of the founder. There is no marketing function, no formalized pipeline management, no structured account management process.

The structural tension at this stage: The founder is the bottleneck in every commercial process simultaneously. he cannot hire fast enough to relieve the bottleneck because the company's revenue is not yet sufficient to fund the team required. he cannot scale the referral pipeline because referrals are dependent on satisfied customers recommending to peers, and the pace of that recommendation is outside her control. Growth is constrained by her personal bandwidth and by the referral network's natural pace.

Stage 2: $10 To $25 Million: First Specialization

How selling, delivery, and service operate: The company begins separating the selling and delivery functions. A dedicated sales hire or small sales team takes over the pipeline development and qualification work, while the founder's commercial role evolves from doing deals to supporting deals. The first marketing investment is typically a website upgrade and basic content production intended to support the sales team's outreach. Customer service is still largely handled by delivery personnel, but a dedicated customer success or account management function may begin to form around the largest accounts.

The structural tension at this stage: The first dedicated sales hire almost always underperforms initial expectations, and understanding why determines whether the company recovers quickly or spends18months repeating the mistake. The most common cause is a mismatch between the salesperson's skills and the selling model: the company hires a product salesperson to sell services, or a corporate enterprise salesperson to sell to the mid-market, or an order-taker to a market that requires a hunter. The founder does not yet have the institutional experience to diagnose this mismatch accurately, so the underperformance is attributed to effort rather than fit.

Stage 3: $25 To $60 Million: The Commercial Architecture Build

How selling, delivery, and service operate: The company now has sufficient scale to support dedicated and separated sales, delivery, and service functions. The sales team has a defined sales process, a CRM system, a pipeline management cadence, and a defined customer profile. The delivery function has a project management or operations management layer that is separate from the sales function. Customer success or account management has become a standalone function with defined responsibilities, defined handoff points from sales and delivery, and defined metrics. The founder's commercial role is primarily strategic and relational: opening doors at the executive level, maintaining the most significant strategic relationships, and closing the largest deals.

The structural tension at this stage: The hand-off process between functions is the most consistently underengineered element of the Stage 3 commercial architecture. When selling, delivery, and service are combined, the transition between them is invisible. When they are separated into distinct functions with distinct teams, the transition becomes a moment of organizational friction: the customer who was handled by one person throughout the early relationship is now handled by three, and the quality of the experience is determined by how well the handoff is designed and executed. Companies that underinvest in the handoff process consistently find that customer satisfaction declines as the company grows, not because the individual functions are worse but because the coordination between them is inadequate.

Stage 4: $60 Million And Beyond: The Mature Commercial Engine

How selling, delivery, and service operate: The commercial organization at this stage is a fully differentiated function with defined sub-specializations within each of its three components. Sales has an inside sales or business development function for prospecting and qualification and an enterprise or field sales function for complex deal management. Delivery or operations has project management, quality management, and continuous improvement disciplines. Customer success has proactive relationship management, reactive issue resolution, and expansion selling capabilities. Marketing has become a genuine investment in brand building, demand generation, and market intelligence rather than a support function for the sales team.

The structural tension at this stage: The Stage 4 challenge is the loss of the founder's commercial energy that powered the company to this scale. The specialized commercial organization is more capable in every individual function than the founder-led combined model was. It is also less cohesive: the knowledge of the customer that was held in one person's head is now distributed across multiple functions and multiple handoffs, and the coordination required to deliver a consistent and high-quality customer experience requires explicit organizational attention that the single-person model never needed.

The Marketing Evolution: From Word of Mouth to Institutional Brand

Marketing in a mid-sized company is the function that most consistently lags the company's commercial scale. It is simultaneously the function most dependent on company size to be effective, the function whose investment returns accrue most slowly, and the function whose value is most difficult to measure in the short-term metrics that dominate mid-sized company management attention.

The result is a predictable pattern: companies underinvest in marketing throughout the growth stage, relying on sales activity and referral networks to drive pipeline, and then discover at 25 to 40 million dollars in revenue that the pipeline is not deep enough, not fast enough, or not diversified enough to support the next growth phase. By the time this discovery happens, the company is trying to build marketing infrastructure while simultaneously managing the revenue shortfall that the insufficient pipeline has produced.

The Referral Economy and Its Limits

Every mid-sized company I have worked with has a moment in its history when referrals were sufficient to support its growth. In the early stage, referrals are not just a marketing strategy, they are the highest-quality pipeline available. Referred customers convert faster, require less selling effort, have shorter sales cycles, and demonstrate higher retention and expansion rates than any other customer acquisition source.

The problem with the referral economy is not its quality. It is its scalability. The referral pipeline is bounded by the size and activity of the satisfied customer base and the founder's personal network. As the company grows, the referral pipeline grows proportionally, but it grows linearly while the company's growth ambitions are typically exponential. At some revenue level, the referral pipeline stops being a sufficient source of new business growth. That level varies by company but it consistently arrives earlier than founders expect.

The founder who has built a 20million-dollar company almost entirely on referrals has a specific commercial risk that the financials do not show: the company's growth is dependent on a pipeline source that cannot be managed, accelerated, or directed. The referred customer comes when a satisfied customer makes a recommendation to a peer who happens to be in the market. The timing of that event is outside the company's control. A company whose entire pipeline is referral-based has no lever to pull when it needs to accelerate growth.

When Formal Marketing Becomes Necessary

The transition from referral-dependent growth to market-built growth typically needs to begin at around 15 to 20 million dollars in revenue, not at 30 million when the pipeline shortage is already visible, but at 15 to 20 million dollars when the foundation of the marketing capability can be built with enough lead time to produce results before they are urgently needed.

Formal marketing in a mid-sized company is not a single function or a single investment. It is a sequence of capability builds whose appropriate form changes as the company scales. The fifteen-million-dollar company needs thought leadership and digital presence, the mechanisms through which it becomes discoverable to prospects who do not yet know the company exists. The 30 million-dollar company needs demand generation, the structured process of moving qualified prospects through the commercial funnel at a velocity the sales team can manage. The 60 million dollar company needs brand architecture, the institutional identity and market positioning that differentiates the company from its competitors in a market segment where multiple credible alternatives exist.

The content investment that supports thought leadership is often the most effective early marketing tool for professional services and technology companies, and the most underutilized by product companies. A company whose executives are writing, speaking, and publishing about the problems their customers face, not about the company's products or services, but about the customer's challenges, builds market credibility that generates qualified inbound interest over a twelve-to-twenty-four-month horizon. The return on this investment is slow. It is also durable: a body of published thought leadership compounds in value over time in a way that paid advertising does not.

Marketing pays off over years. Founders fund it in a panic. Invest while the pipeline is healthy — so the returns arrive before the shortage.

Concentration: The Invisible Risk That Marketing Solves

The customer concentration that accumulates in a mid-sized company's early growth phase is not just a financial risk. It is a commercial structure risk that directly reflects the limits of the referral-based marketing model and the combined role commercial architecture of the early stage.

When the company's customer acquisition is driven entirely by the founder's personal network and referrals from existing customers, the resulting customer portfolio reflects the founder's specific network rather than the company's potential market. The customers are concentrated in the industries, geographies, and organizational profiles that are most represented in the founder's personal relationships. The accounts are typically larger than the market average because the founder's personal access is highest at the senior levels of organizations where he has existing relationships. The resulting portfolio has significant concentration risk embedded in its origin story.

The good news about this concentration is that it is structural and therefore addressable. It is not the result of bad strategic choices, it is the result of good commercial instincts applied to the available resources at the early stage. Addressing it requires building the marketing and sales capabilities that create access to prospects outside the founder's existing network, which is exactly what the formal marketing investment described in the previous section produces.

The practical target for customer concentration management in a mid-sized company approaching a capital event is well-established in the transaction market: no single customer above twenty percent of revenue, and the top five customers below forty-five percent. Getting from the typical early-stage concentration profile, one or two customers above twenty-five percent, top five above sixty percent, to these targets requires two to three years of deliberate new account development that is only possible if the marketing investment that generates new account access was made two to three years earlier.

This is another manifestation of the trailing period asymmetry described in the article on exit preparation: the marketing investment that produces the customer diversification required for a premium transaction valuation must be made two to three years before the transaction, not during the final preparation period. The company that starts building marketing capability at the moment it identifies customer concentration as a transaction risk is the company that will still have the concentration problem when it enters the process.

The Owner's Evolving Commercial Role: The Hardest Transition in Growing a Company

I want to address the owner's commercial role specifically, because across all three selling models and all four stages of commercial evolution, the transition from founder-as-primary-seller to founder-as-commercial-strategist is the single most consequential and most consistently mismanaged transition in mid-sized company growth.

The founder's commercial involvement in the early stage is not just valuable, it is irreplaceable. The founder embodies the company's origin story, its competitive differentiation, and its service commitment in a way that no hired salesperson can replicate. Customers in the early stage are buying the founder as much as they are buying the company. The founder's personal credibility, his direct engagement, his willingness to make commitments and stand behind them personally, these are the commercial assets that build the company's first customer base and establish its market reputation.

The problem is that these same qualities become organizational liabilities at scale. The customers who bought the founder cannot easily be transitioned to institutional account management without friction. The founder who closes every significant deal creates an implicit commitment that every significant customer interaction will involve the founder, which is not a commitment the company can sustain at 40 or 60 million dollars in revenue. The founder whose personal reputation is the company's primary commercial asset has built a company that is worth less to a buyer, because the primary commercial asset leaves with the founder.

Stage	The Owner's Appropriate Commercial Role
$0 to $15M	Primary seller, primary relationship manager, primary service credibility. The founder IS the commercial function. This is appropriate and necessary.
$15 to $35M	Senior deal support on largest opportunities; relationship holder for five to ten most strategic accounts; commercial direction setter for the growing sales team. Beginning the transition away from personal pipeline management.
$35 to $60M	Executive sponsor on top-tier strategic accounts and largest new business opportunities; commercial strategy and talent decisions; customer escalation resource for significant service failures; PR and thought leadership as market positioning.
$60M+	Market positioning and brand; board-level customer relationships at the CEO-to-CEO level; commercial strategy and investment decisions; competitive intelligence and market development. The day-to-day commercial function operates independently.

The transition through these stages is not automatic. It requires the owner to deliberately reduce involvement in activities he is still capable of performing and that still generate positive outcomes, because the organizational cost of her continued involvement, the team that does not develop because the owner is always there, the deals that the salesperson does not learn to close because the owner steps in, exceeds the deal-by-deal value of her direct contribution.

This is, in my experience, the most personally difficult commercial decision a founder makes. he is giving up the activity he is best at, that has produced the company's success, and that he genuinely enjoys, not because the activity has stopped generating value, but because the company's long-term commercial health requires the development of organizational commercial capability that can only be developed if the founder stops doing the thing he does best.

A founder closing every big deal isn't an asset. He's a bottleneck the company hasn't admitted yet.

What a Mature Commercial Architecture Looks Like and Why It Creates Value

The commercial architecture that a mid-sized company should be building toward, in every selling model and at every stage of growth, is one that can generate, qualify, and close new business, deliver on the promises it makes in the selling process, retain and expand the customer base it builds, and build institutional market presence that reduces the company's dependence on any single individual, including the founder.

This architecture has three distinct and separated functions, each with its own talent profile, its own success metrics, and its own management cadence. A company that has built all three, and has built the handoff processes between them that maintain the customer experience quality across all three, has built something that is genuinely valuable, both as a business and as a transaction asset.

A differentiated salesforce whose capability is embedded in repeatable process, documented methodology, and institutional product knowledge rather than in individual relationships. A delivery and operations function whose performance quality is measured, managed, and consistently documented rather than dependent on practitioner reputation. A customer success function whose ability to retain and expand the customer base is driven by proactive relationship management rather than reactive problem-solving.

And supporting all three: a marketing function that builds the institutional identity, the market presence, and the demand generation infrastructure that creates a pipeline independent of the founder's personal network, diverse enough to reduce customer concentration risk, and visible enough in the target market to attract the talent the commercial functions require to grow.

I have built versions of this architecture in the companies I have run, in stages and imperfectly, with the specific mistakes that arise from learning the lessons late rather than early. I have also watched it built in the companies I advise, with the specific advantage of having learned from the prior mistakes. The consistent observation is this: the company that has the mature commercial architecture in place does not just perform better in its market. It is structurally more valuable, because the commercial performance does not depend on any single individual's continued presence, and because the buyer or investor who evaluates it can see a commercial engine that will continue producing results after the founder's role changes.

That architecture is not built in the final two years before a transaction. It is built throughout the company's growth, in the specific transitions I have described. Each transition is difficult. Each produces organizational friction and short-term performance disruption that makes staying in the current model temporarily more attractive than building the next one. And each transition, navigated successfully, produces a company that is meaningfully more capable and more valuable than the one that existed before it.

Commercial architecture compounds. Get the decisions right and advantage builds. Defer them and fragility does.

Summary

The commercial evolution described in this chapter is not a single change. It is a sequence of them, each demanding a different organization, a different talent mix, and a different level of founder involvement than the stage before it. The selling model is not a tactic. It is an expression of the business model itself. The people, cycles, and owner roles required in services, products, and technology are different enough that lessons borrowed from one category often fail in another.

The four stages of commercial evolution create a map of what the company must build if the revenue engine is going to grow beyond the founder's personal network and bandwidth. But the commercial engine is only half the story. What the business earns and what it actually produces in cash are not the same thing. The next chapter picks up that distinction and examines the gap between revenue activity and free cash flow, which is the number that ultimately determines what the company can fund, what it can borrow, and what it is worth.

10

FREE CASH FLOW: THE NUMBER THAT DETERMINES EVERYTHING ELSE

EBITDA IS THE STORY AND FREE CASH FLOW IS THE RECEIPT.

For a mid-sized company navigating growth, managing debt, and eventually approaching a liquidity event, these two numbers are rarely the same, and the gap between them is where the most important management decisions live.

The conversation that most reliably reveals the financial management sophistication of a mid-sized company CEO is not the one about revenue or EBITDA or growth rate. It is the one about free cash flow.

I have had versions of this conversation in every operating and advisory role I have held. I ask the question directly: what did the business generate in free cash flow last year, and how does that compare to what the financial statements showed as profit? The answers I receive span an extraordinary range. Some CEOs answer without hesitation, with specific numbers and a clear articulation of the conversion rate and what drove it. These are almost always the companies that are performing best, managing debt most effectively, and arriving at capital events from a position of strength.

The more common answer is a pause, followed by a pivot to EBITDA. The CEO knows what the business earned. He is less certain what the business produced. And that distinction, between earned and produced, between accounting profit and actual cash, is the most consequential financial management concept available to a mid-sized company owner, and the one most consistently underweighted in the management disciplines of companies I have observed and advised.

Free cash flow is not a sophisticated concept. It is the cash the business generates from operations after paying for the capital expenditures required to maintain and grow the business. It is the money available for debt service, for organic growth investment, for opportunistic acquisitions, for owner distributions, and for the balance sheet health that determines how a lender evaluates the company's creditworthiness and how a buyer evaluates its transaction value. Everything consequential in the financial life of a mid-sized company flows from this single number, or is constrained by it.

This chapter covers the full landscape of free cash flow management for a mid-sized company: its relationship to reported earnings, its role in day to day and week to week cash management, its function as the foundation of debt capacity and debt renewal, its evolution as the business scales, and its central role in the valuation and structure of a liquidity event. At each stage, the goal is the same: to give the CEO who reads it a specific, operational understanding of the number that determines everything else.

Profitable and cash poor is not a contradiction. It's a warning. The gap between earnings and cash is the most important number a CEO can manage.

What Free Cash Flow Is and Why It Differs From Earnings

Free cash flow is calculated simply: operating cash flow minus capital expenditures. Operating cash flow is net income adjusted for non cash charges (primarily depreciation and amortization) and changes in working capital. Capital expenditures are the investments required to maintain the company's productive capacity and fund its growth. The result is the cash that is genuinely free, available for any use the company chooses, after the business has funded its own ongoing operation.

The gap between EBITDA and free cash flow has three primary drivers, and understanding each one is essential to managing the metric rather than simply reporting it.

Driver One: Working Capital Consumption

Working capital, the difference between current assets and current liabilities, primarily the net of accounts receivable, inventory, and accounts payable, consumes cash when it expands and releases cash when it contracts. A growing mid-sized company almost always has expanding working capital: more accounts receivable as revenue grows, more inventory if the product requires it, and a payables balance that rarely grows as fast as the receivable balance in a company that is managing vendor relationships carefully.

The specific implication is one that consistently surprises founders who encounter it for the first time: a rapidly growing company can have strong EBITDA margins and consume significant cash simply because the growth is outpacing the working capital cycle. A company that grows revenue by 20 percent in a year and maintains sixty day average receivables days has tied up approximately three months of additional revenue in working capital. On a 30 million dollar base, that is five million dollars of cash consumed by growth, entirely outside the income statement, invisible in the EBITDA calculation, and entirely real in the bank account.

Driver Two: Capital Expenditure Requirements

EBITDA adds back depreciation, treating it as a non cash charge that does not represent real economic cost. For a business whose capital equipment can be maintained and upgraded at a cost equal to or below its annual depreciation, this addback is approximately correct. For a business whose growth requires capital investment significantly above depreciation, the EBITDA number flatters the actual cash generation of the business.

The capital intensity of the business, measured as capital expenditures as a percentage of revenue, is one of the most important determinants of free cash flow conversion rate. A professional services business with minimal fixed asset requirements may convert 80 to 90 percent of EBITDA into free cash flow. A manufacturing business investing in equipment for growth may convert for 60 percent. A technology business in infrastructure build out may convert less. These differences are not incidental. They determine how much capital the company needs to fund its growth, how much debt service it can support, and ultimately what multiple a buyer is justified in paying for it.

Driver Three: Tax and Interest Cash Costs

EBITDA excludes interest expense and taxes by definition. Free cash flow does not. For a mid-sized company carrying meaningful debt, which is the typical condition for a company that has used debt to fund growth or acquisition, the interest expense line is a substantial cash cost that does not appear in the EBITDA comparison. A company with four million dollars of EBITDA and one million dollars of annual interest expense has three million dollars of pre tax earnings from which taxes must be paid before a dollar of genuinely free cash is available. The CEO who manages the business to EBITDA without tracking the cash impact of interest and taxes is managing to a number that consistently overstates actual cash generation.

The Daily Discipline: Managing Cash Flow in the Short Term

Every mid-sized company CEO who has run a business through a tight cash period understands something that the quarterly financial review does not capture: the management of free cash flow happens at the weekly level, not the quarterly level. The decisions about when to pay vendors, how aggressively to collect receivables, whether to pull forward or defer a capital expenditure, and whether to draw on the credit facility to fund a growth opportunity are made in real time, with imperfect information, under the pressure of competing demands on a limited cash balance.

These decisions are neither trivial nor purely operational. They are financial strategy expressed in daily execution, and the aggregate of these daily decisions determines the company's actual cash position, its credit facility utilization, and its relationship with the lenders and vendors who represent the company's external financial ecosystem.

The Receivables Collection Discipline

The most consistent source of working capital leakage in mid-sized companies is undisciplined receivables collection. Average receivable days that drift above the contracted payment terms represent cash that the company has earned but not yet collected, cash that is funding the customer's business rather than the company's. On a 20 million dollar annual revenue base, the difference between 40 day average collection days and 60 day average collection days is approximately one million dollars of working capital, cash that either sits in the company's account or in the customer's.

The collection discipline is not just about sending invoices and following up on late payments. It is about the commercial relationship terms negotiated at the point of sale, the invoicing accuracy that determines whether payment is delayed by disputes rather than by customer cash management, and the escalation process for accounts that extend beyond terms without explanation. I have found in every company I have managed that a 30 day receivables management improvement program, focused on invoice accuracy, terms compliance, and systematic follow up, reliably releases between five and 10 percent of annual revenue in working capital. On a 30million dollar company, that is one and a half to three million dollars of cash generated from better process rather than from growth.

The Payables Management Trade Off

The management of accounts payable involves a specific trade off that mid-sized company CEOs navigate differently depending on their financial philosophy and their current cash position. Extending payables, paying vendors at or near the end of their contracted terms rather than early, is a legitimate working capital management technique that preserves cash at no cost when the vendor relationship can sustain it. Taking early payment discounts, the common '2/10 net 30' term that offers a two percent discount for payment within 10 days, represents an annualized return of approximately 36 percent, which exceeds the cost of any credit facility the company would use to fund the alternative. For a company with available credit facility capacity, taking every available early payment discount is one of the highest return capital allocation decisions available.

The trade off becomes more complex when the company's cash position is constrained. Extending payables conserves cash in the short term but damages vendor relationships over time, can trigger credit terms restrictions that make the supply chain more expensive, and signals to the financial community that the company is managing its cash flow actively, a signal that lenders monitoring covenant compliance read with attention. I have found that maintaining a strict discipline of paying vendors within terms, not early and not late, while extracting every available early payment discount produces the best combination of vendor relationship quality, cash conservation, and financial presentation quality.

The Thirteen Week Forecast as a Management Instrument

The management tool that does more to improve daily and weekly cash decision quality than any other is the 13 week rolling cash flow forecast. This is not a financial model, it is an operational instrument. Updated every week, it projects the company's cash receipts, cash disbursements, and resulting bank balance for the next 13 weeks, week by week. It shows specifically which weeks have positive net cash positions and which have negative ones, which customer payments are expected and when, and what the credit facility utilization will be at any point in the forecast horizon.

The 13 week forecast does three things simultaneously. It identifies cash shortfalls before they occur, giving management the two to four week lead time required to address them through accelerated collection, deferred expenditure, or credit facility draw rather than through emergency measures. It improves collection discipline because the weekly cash receipt projections create accountability for the collection team's performance against forecast. And it provides the lender with the specific, current format cash management data that most credit agreements require and that, when provided proactively and regularly, builds the lender relationship quality that produces flexibility during covenant stress periods.

Without a 13-week cash forecast, you aren't managing cash. You're reacting to it.

Free Cash Flow as the Engine of Growth: How It Changes as the Business Scales

The role of free cash flow in funding growth changes fundamentally as a mid-sized company moves through its revenue scaling phases, and understanding these changes is the prerequisite for making good capital allocation decisions at each stage.

The Early Growth Phase ($5M to $20M): Preservation and Proof

At the early growth stage, free cash flow is primarily a survival metric and a proof of concept signal. The company is generating FCF, but the amount is modest relative to the capital requirements of the growth opportunity. The primary cash management discipline is preservation: ensuring that the business never runs below a minimum operating cash buffer, that the credit facility is used for its intended purpose of funding working capital fluctuations rather than operating losses, and that the free cash flow trend is consistently positive.

The proof of concept function of FCF in this phase is its role in demonstrating to lenders and potential future investors that the business model generates real cash from operations rather than only accounting profits. A company that has been generating positive and improving free cash flow for three consecutive years has established a financial track record that is fundamentally more credible to a capital provider than one that has been generating EBITDA without demonstrating cash conversion. This track record is being built during the early growth phase, whether the management team is intentionally building it or not.

The Mid Growth Phase ($20M to $60M): Allocation and Leverage

At the mid growth phase, free cash flow transitions from a survival and proof metric to a capital allocation resource. The company is generating enough FCF to make meaningful choices about where that capital goes: into organic growth investments (hiring, marketing, product development), into debt reduction that improves the balance sheet for a future refinancing, into working capital improvements that improve the FCF generation rate itself, or into distributions to the owner.

The capital allocation discipline at this stage is the most consequential financial management responsibility of the mid growth CEO. I have observed two consistent allocation errors in companies at this phase. The first is over distribution: the owner, recognizing that the business is generating real cash, increases personal distributions at a pace that limits the company's ability to fund organic growth from internal cash generation, increasing reliance on the credit facility for growth investment that could have been funded from FCF. The second is under investment in working capital improvement: the company continues funding growth with external capital while leaving significant working capital optimization available in the receivables and inventory cycle, because the working capital opportunity is less visible than the growth investment opportunity.

The Scaling Phase ($60M+): Strategic Capital and Institutional Quality

At the scaling phase, free cash flow becomes the basis of a strategic capital conversation rather than an operational cash management conversation. The company's FCF generation capacity is the primary asset it brings to conversations with institutional lenders, growth equity investors, and potential acquirors. At this scale, the FCF discussion shifts from how much does the company generate to how consistently does it generate it, what is the quality and predictability of the generation, and what is the conversion rate trend over the prior three years.

The FCF conversion rate, free cash flow as a percentage of EBITDA, is the single most informative ratio available to a sophisticated capital provider evaluating a scaling mid sizde company. A company with a 70 percent FCF conversion rate, generating 70 cents of free cash for every dollar of EBITDA, is a fundamentally different investment from one with a 40 percent conversion rate, even if the EBITDA is identical. The high conversion business has lower working capital requirements, lower capital intensity, and a more cash generative business model. It can service more debt per dollar of EBITDA, it can self fund more of its growth, and it will command a higher multiple from a buyer who understands what the conversion rate means for the sustainability and quality of the earnings.

EBITDA is the headline. Cash conversion is the fine print. Buyers and lenders read the fine print.

Free Cash Flow as the Foundation of Debt Capacity and Debt Renewal

When a lender evaluates a mid-sized company's creditworthiness, whether at the initial underwriting of a new credit facility or at the annual renewal of an existing one, the primary analytical lens is the relationship between the company's free cash flow and its debt service obligations. Not EBITDA. Not revenue growth. Free cash flow.

The debt service coverage ratio, DSCR, defined as the company's annual free cash flow divided by its required annual debt service payments of principal and interest, is the metric that most directly determines whether a lender will provide or renew a credit facility, at what size, and at what price. A DSCR above 1.25 means the company generates 25 percent more free cash flow than required to service its debt in every period which is the minimum coverage level most institutional lenders require as a financial maintenance covenant. A DSCR below 1.00 means the company cannot service its debt from its own free cash flow, a covenant violation found In virtually every credit agreement and the condition that triggers the lender's right to demand accelerated repayment.

The practical implication for a mid-sized company CEO managing through a debt renewal is direct: the 12 months of financial performance preceding the renewal negotiation determine the renewal terms with substantially more force than any management presentation, investment banker engagement, or lender relationship. A company that arrives at its annual credit review with three consecutive quarters of DSCR above 1.25, improving free cash flow conversion, and a 13 week forecast showing comfortable coverage through the next quarter has a renewal conversation. A company that arrives with DSCR between 1.00 and 1.25, declining FCF conversion, and no forward cash visibility has a renegotiation conversation under stress.

I have been through both versions of this conversation from the borrower's side. The leverage differential between the two is not marginal. In the renewal conversation, the borrower is negotiating the specific terms, the rate, the covenants, the basket provisions, from a position of demonstrated performance. In the renegotiation under stress, the borrower is defending the right to continue accessing a facility whose terms the lender now has the contractual standing to revise. Every borrower who has experienced the second version understands with clarity that the management decisions that determined which conversation occurred were made 12 to 18 months before the renewal date, not in the week before it.

Free Cash Flow Position Heading into Renewal	What the Lender Sees	Renewal Outcome
DSCR consistently above 1.35x, FCF conversion improving, 13 week forecast current	Low risk borrower with disciplined cash management and adequate coverage buffer. Proactive financial reporting signals management quality.	Favorable rate renewal, expanded covenant headroom, potential for facility increase or term extension at borrower's request.
DSCR between 1.10x and 1.35x, FCF conversion flat, limited forward visibility	Adequate but not comfortable coverage. Management may be optimizing for EBITDA rather than cash. Limited ability to absorb a negative performance quarter.	Renewal at similar terms; possible covenant tightening; increased reporting requirements. Borrower has limited negotiating leverage.
DSCR approaching 1.00x, FCF conversion declining, no 13 week forecast	Covenant stress risk. Lender begins portfolio management posture. Draws on credit facility may be scrutinized for purpose and sustainability.	Conditional renewal with restructured covenants; potential requirement for financial advisor engagement; reduced facility size possible. Borrower is negotiating from weakness.
DSCR below 1.00x or covenant breach	Impaired credit. Lender has contractual remedies. Relationship is in workout mode regardless of how it is characterized.	Waiver negotiation, forbearance agreement, or acceleration of maturity. Personal guarantee exposure becomes active. Transaction may be forced rather than chosen.

Free Cash Flow in Valuation and Liquidity Events: The Number Behind the Multiple

In the prior chapter, I have described the role of EBITDA in transaction valuation and the importance of EBITDA quality from a buyer's perspective. I want to be specific here about the relationship between free cash flow and the multiple a buyer applies to EBITDA in a liquidity event, because this relationship is the most financially significant implication of FCF management available to a mid-sized company owner.

Private equity buyers and strategic acquirors value mid-sized companies using a multiple of EBITDA as the primary transaction metric. But the multiple is not fixed. It is a judgment that reflects the buyer's assessment of the quality and sustainability of the earnings being valued. And the single most important determinant of earnings quality, from a buyer's perspective, is the FCF conversion rate: how much of the reported EBITDA actually becomes free cash flow that a new owner can use.

A company with four million dollars of EBITDA and a 70 percent FCF conversion rate generates 2.8 million dollars of free cash flow annually. A company with the same four million dollars of EBITDA and a 40 percent conversion rate generates 1.6 million dollars. These two companies are not worth the same amount despite having identical EBITDA. The first is worth more because the cash available to the new owner for debt service, reinvestment, and return of capital is 75 percent higher. A rational buyer who understands this will pay a meaningfully higher multiple for the first company and a lower multiple for the second, even if the management presentation for both features the same headline EBITDA number.

The three working capital elements that most directly determine FCF conversion quality, and that a buyer's diligence team examines with specific attention, are receivables days outstanding, inventory turns, and payables days outstanding. A business with receivable days improving toward industry best practice, inventory turns at or above the sector median, and payables days within contracted terms has working capital discipline that is visible to a buyer and valued at a premium. A business with receivable days drifting above contracted terms, inventory accumulation, and extended payables has working capital problems that a buyer will price as a cash flow risk.

The FCF Bridge in Transaction Documentation

The most effective single document a seller can prepare in advance of a liquidity event process, beyond the quality of earnings analysis itself, is a three year FCF bridge: a written reconciliation from EBITDA to free cash flow for each of the prior three fiscal years, with each component of the conversion (working capital change, capex, interest, taxes) clearly documented and explained. This document does three things simultaneously.

It demonstrates that management understands the distinction between earnings and cash, a signal of financial sophistication that sophisticated buyers notice and value. It provides the buyer's diligence team with a head start on their own FCF analysis, reducing the diligence timeline and the period of uncertainty before the buyer's financial assessment is complete. And it gives the seller the analytical foundation to defend the FCF conversion rate during the valuation negotiation, to explain specifically why the conversion rate in a year when working capital expanded reflects growth investment rather than structural working capital inefficiency.

FCF and Deal Structure: The Earnout and the Working Capital Peg

Free cash flow appears in transaction documentation in two specific structural elements that every seller should understand before entering a process.

The working capital peg is the specific amount of net working capital that the seller is required to leave in the business at closing. The peg is typically set at the historical average working capital balance, and the purchase price is adjusted upward or downward depending on whether the actual working capital at closing is above or below the peg. A seller who manages working capital down aggressively in the months before closing, accelerating collections, extending payables, and reducing inventory below operating levels, to generate a pre closing cash distribution will find that the peg adjustment returns that cash to the buyer through a lower effective purchase price. The working capital peg neutralizes the most common working capital manipulation in transaction processes, and sellers who attempt it consistently discover the mechanism during the closing adjustment calculation.

The earnout structure, when it appears, is frequently tied to the company's FCF generation in the post closing period rather than to revenue or EBITDA. FCF based earnouts are structurally more buyer friendly because they incorporate the working capital and capex discipline that pure EBITDA earnouts do not. A seller who has managed FCF actively in the years before the transaction is better positioned to earn out an FCF based earnout target than a seller whose FCF management has been passive, because the FCF management discipline that earned the earnout target is the same discipline that the seller has been applying for the prior three years.

Six Principles for FCF Management Across the Company's Life

The following principles consolidate the article's practical content into a framework that can be applied at any stage of the company's development. They are organized in the sequence of their importance: the first principle is the foundation on which the others rest.

Principle 1: Measure Free Cash Flow Monthly, Not Quarterly

The company that measures FCF quarterly is making cash allocation decisions on 60 to 90 day old information. The company that measures it monthly can identify working capital deterioration, capex overruns, and FCF conversion rate changes in real time, when the management response options are still abundant rather than limited. Monthly FCF tracking, supported by the 13 week rolling forecast at the operational level, produces a financial management environment in which the CEO is ahead of cash events rather than behind them. This is the single change in financial management practice that consistently produces the fastest and most significant improvement in FCF management quality across the mid-sized companies I have worked with.

Principle 2: Set A Minimum FCF Conversion Rate Target and Manage to It

The FCF conversion rate, free cash flow as a percentage of EBITDA, should be an explicit management target rather than an observed outcome. For most mid-sized service businesses, a conversion rate above 60 percent is achievable with disciplined working capital management. For capital intensive product businesses, above 50 percent is a reasonable target. For technology businesses in growth mode, above 40 percent. Setting the target makes the conversion rate a managed variable rather than a residual. Management teams that track conversion rate quarterly, identify the drivers of quarterly variation, and set improvement plans when the rate falls below target consistently outperform those that manage to EBITDA alone.

Principle 3: Treat Receivables Days as a Performance Metric, Not an Accounting Observation

Receivables days outstanding should appear in the company's weekly management reporting alongside revenue and gross margin. The person responsible for billing and collections should have a personal performance metric tied to receivables days, with a defined target, a defined tolerance for variation above the target, and a defined escalation protocol for accounts that extend beyond terms. The CEO who reviews receivables days weekly alongside revenue will, over time, produce a collection discipline that generates more working capital improvement than most growth initiatives produce in revenue. This is not a financial management insight. It is an operational management choice.

Principle 4: Use The Credit Facility for Working Capital, Not Operations

The most common sign of FCF management breakdown in a mid-sized company is a revolving credit facility that is drawn at or near its maximum utilization for the majority of the year. A properly functioning revolving credit facility should follow the working capital cycle: drawn up when working capital is high (during growth periods or seasonal peaks) and paid down when working capital releases. A facility that is permanently drawn is not funding working capital fluctuations. It is funding operating cash deficiency, which means the business is not generating enough free cash flow from operations to fund itself without the credit facility as a permanent subsidy. This condition is a warning signal that the lender will eventually act on, and the CEO who identifies and addresses it before the lender does retains control of the resolution.

Principle 5: Build The FCF Bridge Before the Banker Asks for It

The three year FCF bridge, the documented reconciliation from EBITDA to free cash flow covering the prior three fiscal years, should be built as a standard element of the company's annual financial reporting package, not as a transaction preparation document. A company that has been building and refining this bridge annually for three years arrives at a capital event with a document that is both more complete and more credible than one prepared specifically for the transaction. It also arrives with management that has thought carefully about the drivers of FCF conversion rate for three years, which is the analytical foundation for the valuation defense conversations that every transaction requires.

Principle 6: Manage FCF Explicitly in the Two Years Before a Liquidity Event

In the two years before a contemplated capital event, FCF management deserves the same level of explicit management attention as EBITDA preparation. Specifically: the working capital cycle should be optimized to its best achievable level so that the trailing 12 month

FCF conversion rate reflects genuine business model quality rather than cyclical working capital variation. The capex budget should be reviewed against its strategic justification, with discretionary capex deferred to the post close period where possible. The receivables collection discipline should be at its peak performance level. And the 13 week forecast should be provided to the lender proactively and regularly in the 18 months before the process, building the lender relationship quality and financial transparency that produces refinancing flexibility at a moment when flexibility may be required.

The Number Behind Every Other Number

I want to close with the observation that ties every section of this article together, because it is the insight that took me the longest to fully internalize and that I have watched produce the most significant management improvements in the companies I have led and advised.

Every consequential financial outcome in the life of a mid-sized company is either produced or constrained by free cash flow: the ability to service and renew debt; the ability to fund organic growth without diluting ownership; the ability to survive a revenue shortfall without a covenant crisis; the ability to make an acquisition when the opportunity arises; the ability to distribute wealth to the owner who built the company; the ability to arrive at a transaction with a balance sheet that supports a premium multiple rather than requiring a structural discount.

All of these outcomes trace back to the same question: does the business generate more cash from operations than it consumes, by enough margin and with enough consistency, to fund the ambitions of its owner and the confidence of its capital providers?

The answer to that question is not fixed. It is the product of specific management decisions made over time: the collection discipline applied to receivables, the capital expenditure choices made against a clear FCF impact framework, the credit facility managed against its intended purpose, and the working capital optimized rather than accepted as a residual. None of these decisions requires exceptional financial sophistication. All of them require consistent attention to a metric that most mid-sized company management systems underweight in favor of the income statement metrics that are easier to see and more commonly discussed.

The CEO who manages free cash flow with the same intensity he brings to revenue and EBITDA management is not doing something exotic. he is managing the complete financial picture of her business, the picture that lenders, investors, and buyers use when they determine what the business is worth and what they are willing to offer for it. he is managing the number that determines everything else.

Revenue is what you sold. EBITDA is what you earned. Free cash flow is what you produced. Capital providers weigh all three. So should you.

Summary

This chapter lays out free cash flow as a full management discipline rather than a line item reviewed after the fact. It traces the gap between earnings and cash back to working capital, capital intensity, taxes, and interest. It moves into the weekly mechanics of collections, payables, and the 13 week forecast that turns reactive cash management into proactive control. It then follows free cash flow into the lender conversation, the growth capital conversation, and finally the transaction conversation, where conversion rate becomes part of the valuation logic itself.

The commercial engine generates the revenue. Free cash flow determines what that revenue becomes once debt service, growth investment, and owner return are taken into account. Together they create the platform on which the outside world evaluates the company. The next chapter shifts explicitly to that outside perspective and asks what a sophisticated buyer sees when they look at the business, often more clearly than the owner does from the inside.

11

THE ACQUIROR'S VIEW

BEST OUTCOMES DON'T GO TO THE BEST BUSINESSES, THEY GO TO THE BEST-PREPARED ONES, YEARS IN ADVANCE.

I have been on both sides of the acquisition table enough times to know that sellers and buyers are looking at the same business through fundamentally different lenses. The seller sees what he built. The buyer sees what he is underwriting.

Those two views are almost never the same. And the gap between them, the distance between what the owner believes his business is worth and what a sophisticated acquiror is prepared to pay for it, is almost never about the quality of the underlying business. It is about preparation. Specifically, the absence of it.

Over the course of my career, as a CEO who built and exited companies, as a chairman who oversaw them through ownership transitions, and now as a principal investor and operating advisor who regularly evaluates acquisition targets, I have observed a pattern with enough consistency to state it as a finding rather than an opinion: the founders who achieve the best outcomes from a liquidity event are not the ones with the best businesses. They are the ones who understood, three to five years before the transaction, how a sophisticated buyer would evaluate their business, and who ran their companies accordingly.

The ones who achieve mediocre outcomes are not running worse businesses. They are running unprepared ones. Anyone can try to sell a company. A prepared owner is far more likely to achieve full value. The difference between those two sentences is everything this article is about.

The best exits don't go to the best businesses. They go to the founders who saw the company through a buyer's eyes years before the buyer arrived.

The Buyer's Lens Is Not the Owner's Lens

Let me describe what happens when my team and I evaluate an acquisition target in the $15M to $150M enterprise value range. It is not the process that most sellers imagine.

The seller imagines that buyers are primarily evaluating the company's historical financial performance, the revenue trend, the EBITDA margin, the growth rate. He has spent months preparing the financial presentation. The numbers are accurate. The story they tell is a good one. He is reasonably confident that a buyer will look at those numbers and arrive at a valuation close to his expectation.

What we are actually doing is something quite different. We are not trying to understand the company's history. We are trying to understand what the company will do after we own it. We are evaluating the probability that the financial performance of the past three years will continue, improve, or deteriorate in the three years after we close. We are not buying the rearview mirror. We are underwriting the windshield.

That distinction changes everything about what we examine and what we value. The financial statements tell us what the machine produced. We want to understand how the machine works, whether it is running at its full capability, whether the performance is embedded in organizational systems or in the personal presence of two or three key individuals, and what we would need to do differently, or not do at all, to sustain and improve it after the transaction closes.

The five elements we examine in every acquisition, normalized EBITDA, management depth, revenue quality, competitive moat, and financial reporting quality, are not items on a checklist. They are the dimensions of a forward probability assessment. Each one represents a specific question about what the business will do in the future. Each one affects the price we are prepared to pay and the structure we are prepared to offer.

More importantly for the seller: each one can be prepared for. Each one responds to specific, deliberate management actions taken before the transaction process begins. The founder who understands this early enough has a significant advantage over the founder who discovers it in the middle of a diligence process, when it is too late to do anything about it.

Why Three to Five Years Is Not Cautious: It Is Necessary

When I suggest to founders that serious exit preparation begins three to five years before the desired transaction, the response is almost always the same. They understand the concept intellectually. They do not act on it with the urgency the timeline requires, because five years feels distant and the operational demands of today feel immediate.

This is the most expensive mistake a founder can make. Let me explain specifically why.

The five elements I described above, normalized EBITDA, management depth, revenue quality, competitive moat, and financial reporting quality, do not improve on a transaction timeline. They improve on an operational timeline. The changes required to optimize them are not presentation changes. They are business changes. And business changes take time to produce financial results that are visible in the trailing performance window that sophisticated buyers weight most heavily.

Consider normalized EBITDA. A company with owner dependent cost structures, above market compensation, personal expenses run through the business, related party arrangements that obscure true operating costs, cannot normalize those elements in the six months before a transaction without the normalization appearing cosmetic rather than structural. A buyer who sees a company whose EBITDA jumped by two margin points in the year before the sale will apply a skeptic's discount to the normalized figure. The same normalization applied consistently over three years is simply the company's actual operating economics. There is nothing to discount.

Consider management depth. Building a management team with genuine independent capability, executives who can run their functions without the founder's daily involvement, takes time. Not because the people are unavailable, but because the organizational habits, decision-making processes, and cultural expectations that make a team genuinely independent cannot be installed in six months. They are built through repeated demonstration, through the founder's consistent willingness to let the team handle what the team is capable of handling, and through the accumulation of a track record that gives the buyer confidence that the performance will continue after the transition.

Anyone can try to sell a company. A prepared owner is far more likely to achieve full value.

Three to five years is not a conservative estimate of the preparation required. It is the minimum. The founders who achieve the best outcomes have typically been preparing, whether they called it that or not, for longer. They have been running their businesses with the discipline, the financial rigor, and the organizational depth that a sophisticated buyer requires, not because they were thinking about an exit, but because those disciplines are also what produces a better run, more valuable company in the present.

The practical implication is direct: if you are reading this article and thinking about a transaction in the next three to five years, the preparation begins today. Not when the investment banker is engaged. Not when the initial inquiries arrive. Today.

The Five Elements Sophisticated Buyers Examine

I want to go through each of the five elements in specific terms, because the standard descriptions of what buyers look for are almost always too abstract to be actionable. I want founders to understand not just what we examine but why each element matters to the forward probability assessment we are constructing, and specifically what actions taken today will improve each element's contribution to that assessment.

Element 1: Normalized EBITDA

The first element is normalized EBITDA, the true recurring earnings of the business, adjusted for the costs that a new owner would not incur and the revenues that a new owner could not rely on.

Every private company in the $15M to $150M range has a gap between its reported EBITDA and its normalized EBITDA. The gap is not fraud. It is the accumulated result of how owner managed businesses are legitimately run: compensation structures that compensate the owner at above market rates because the business can afford it; personal expenses that flow through the company for legitimate tax reasons; advisory and consulting fees paid to related parties at above market rates; one-time items that appear on the income statement with enough regularity that they have effectively become permanent costs.

When my team reconstructs normalized EBITDA, we are not looking for problems. We are looking for the true economic earnings that the business is capable of producing for a new owner who does not have the same personal cost structure. In a well-managed $30M revenue company, this gap is typically 15 to 25 percent of reported EBITDA. In less disciplined situations, it can be 40 percent or more.

The owner who begins normalizing his business's economics three years before a transaction, who restructures compensation to market rates, who removes personal costs from the business, who eliminates the related party arrangements that inflate the cost structure, presents a buyer with a company whose reported and normalized EBITDA are essentially the same number. There is nothing to reconstruct. There is no discount to apply. The earnings are what they appear to be. That confidence is worth a significant multiple premium.

Element 2: Management Depth

The second element is what I consider the most consequential and the most frequently underestimated. Management depth is the degree to which the company's performance is the product of its organizational systems and its management team's independent capability, rather than the product of the founder's personal presence, relationships, and judgment.

When we evaluate management depth, we are asking a single underlying question: if the founder exits on the day of closing, what happens to this business in year two? The answer to that question is the most important variable in our valuation model. A business whose year-two performance is independent of the founder's presence is worth significantly more than one that requires the founder to stay for three years under an employment agreement before we can know whether it will hold.

The diagnostic we apply is specific. We map the five to seven activities that most directly produce the company's competitive outcomes. For each activity, we assess whether the leader of that activity could be replaced within 90 days without material performance deterioration. If the answer is no for more than one or two activities, the business has a key man problem that will be reflected in the purchase price, the deal structure, or both.

The founder who addresses this element proactively, who builds a genuine management bench, who institutionalizes his own knowledge into organizational processes, who creates a decision-making culture that does not require his personal validation at every step, is not just making his company more valuable at exit. He is making his company better to own and operate today. The organizational depth built to impress a future buyer is the same depth that makes the company more resilient, more scalable, and more capable of executing the strategic initiatives that will produce its next phase of growth.

Element 3: Revenue Quality

The third element is revenue quality, the assessment of how durable, how predictable, and how concentrated the company's revenue base is.

We value revenue on a spectrum. At the high end: contracted, recurring revenue from customers who have been buying from this company for years, whose purchases are governed by agreements that require advance notice to terminate, and whose individual share of total revenue is small enough that no single defection represents a material business risk. At the low end: transactional revenue from a concentrated customer base with no contractual commitment, where the top three customers represent forty percent of revenue and the relationships are managed personally by the founder.

Both ends of this spectrum can produce identical EBITDA margins. They produce very different valuations. The high-quality revenue base supports a higher multiple because the forward probability of that revenue continuing is higher. The concentrated, founder-dependent revenue base requires a discount because the buyer is assuming a risk that the financials do not explicitly show.

The actions required to improve revenue quality are among the most operationally valuable investments a founder can make regardless of exit intentions: converting transactional customer relationships to contractual ones; systematically reducing customer concentration by developing new accounts; transitioning the key customer relationships from personal founder management to institutional account management so that they survive an ownership transition. Three years of deliberate effort on these dimensions produces a revenue quality profile that a buyer reads as durable. Six months of effort produces a profile that a buyer reads with skepticism.

One specific metric I examine in every acquisition: net revenue retention, the percentage of prior-year revenue retained from existing customers, including the impact of expansions and contractions. A company with net revenue retention consistently above one hundred percent is growing its existing customer base without new customer acquisition. That is a signal of genuine competitive strength and customer satisfaction that no presentation can manufacture.

Element 4: Competitive Moat

The fourth element is competitive moat, the specific, articulable reason why this company's competitive position is defensible against the competition that will exist three years after we own it, not just the competition that exists today.

I have sat through hundreds of management presentations in which the founder describes the company's competitive advantages with genuine conviction. The advantages are real. What is frequently missing is the institutional architecture that makes them durable. A company whose competitive advantage is 'our people' has a advantage that is contingent on those specific people remaining employed. A company whose competitive advantage is 'our customer relationships' has an advantage that is contingent on those specific relationships surviving the ownership transition. A company whose competitive advantage is embedded in its documented processes, its proprietary systems, and its organizational routines has an advantage that persists regardless of individual personnel changes.

The moat I am most willing to pay a premium for is the one that does not walk out the door with any single individual. The moat I discount most heavily is the one that is embodied in the founder's personal network, judgment, or energy, not because those things are not genuinely valuable, but because I cannot underwrite their continuation after the transition.

The practical implication for founders: the competitive advantages that are most valuable to you personally, the relationships you have built, the market knowledge you have accumulated, the customer trust you have earned, must be converted into institutional assets before the transaction. Documented account management processes. Written competitive intelligence. Relationship transition protocols. The founder who does this work converts his personal competitive capital into organizational capital, which is the form in which it generates the highest value at exit.

Element 5: Financial Reporting Quality

The fifth element is financial reporting quality, the degree to which the company's financial statements accurately, completely, and consistently represent its economic reality in a form that a sophisticated external reviewer can rely on without significant reconstruction.

This element is the one that most surprises founders when I describe how heavily it influences the valuation. Financial reporting quality is not about having audited statements, though audited statements help. It is about the degree of confidence a buyer can have that the numbers are what they appear to be, that the revenue recognition is consistent, that the cost classifications are appropriate, and that the financial reporting infrastructure will support the management oversight requirements of a new owner.

A company with high financial reporting quality compresses the diligence timeline. There are fewer questions, fewer reconciliations, fewer adjustments to the financial model. The buyer's quality of earnings team moves faster and produces a report that confirms rather than revises the initial financial picture. That compression creates a better transaction experience and reduces the probability of a late-stage price adjustment, the most common and most demoralizing moment in any sale process.

A company with low financial reporting quality, inconsistent revenue recognition, commingled personal and business expenses, management reporting that is months behind the operational reality, financial statements that have never been independently reviewed, creates an information risk premium that buyers price into the transaction. It also creates a diligence environment in which every question generates three more, the timeline extends, and the probability of a price chip or a deal failure increases substantially.

The three-year preparation investment for this element is specific: commission reviewed financial statements for each of the three years before the intended transaction; implement a monthly close that produces financial statements within 10 days of month-end; build a management reporting package that tracks the operational and financial metrics that will matter most to a buyer; and document the revenue recognition policy in writing, consistently applied, before the diligence process asks for it.

What the Gap Between Presented and Prepared Actually Costs

I want to be direct about the financial consequences of the gap between a company that is merely presented for sale and one that is genuinely prepared.

In my experience evaluating acquisitions in the \$15M to \$150M enterprise value range, the valuation difference between a well-prepared company and an unprepared company with identical underlying financial performance is consistently in the range of one to two EBITDA turns. On a company generating \$5M of normalized

EBITDA, that is $5M to $10M of enterprise value, on a transaction that the seller will probably complete only once in his life.

This premium is not the result of a better financial presentation or a more compelling investment banker pitch. It is the result of the buyer's confidence that the five elements I described above are genuinely present, that the earnings are real and sustainable, that the management team will perform independently, that the revenue base is durable, that the competitive position is defensible, and that the financial reporting can be relied upon without significant reconstruction.

The costs of being unprepared extend beyond the purchase price. An unprepared company takes longer to sell because the diligence process is more complicated. A longer sale process creates more organizational disruption, more customer and employee uncertainty, and more opportunities for the transaction to fall apart before closing. Deals that fail after significant management time and emotional investment have been committed to the process are among the most damaging events in a founder's professional life. They are also, in my observation, disproportionately concentrated among companies that were not genuinely prepared when the process began.

The Unprepared Sale	The Prepared Sale
Discovered normalization issues reduce purchase price in late diligence	Normalized EBITDA and reported EBITDA are essentially aligned from day one
Key-man dependency requires employment agreement and earnout to bridge valuation gap	Management depth demonstrated over 3 years supports clean close with minimal transition requirements
Customer concentration creates revenue risk discount in buyer's model	Diversified, contractual revenue base supports full multiple application
Founder-dependent competitive advantages require personal stay to be underwritten	Institutional competitive advantages transfer with the organization
Financial reporting inconsistencies extend diligence timeline and create price chipping	Clean reporting compresses diligence, supports full price confidence, and closes on schedule

The Preparation Framework: Starting Three to Five Years Out

The following framework is what I recommend to the founders and CEOs I work with when they begin thinking seriously about a transaction. It is organized around the five elements, with specific actions and a rough timeline for each. It is not a project plan. It is a discipline, a set of management practices that should be embedded in the way the company is run, not bolted on in the final months before a sale.

Years One and Two: Build the Foundation

The first two years are about building the organizational and financial infrastructure that will generate the trailing performance a buyer will rely on. No amount of preparation in year five compensates for weak fundamentals in years three and four.

Start with the bandwidth audit I described in an earlier article. Identify the management responsibilities that must be transferred from the founder to the organizational infrastructure before a transaction can close cleanly. Begin building the management bench, not the management bench the company has today, but the one it will need when the founder exits. Invest in the A-players for the two or three critical roles that are currently founder-dependent.

Simultaneously, begin the financial reporting normalization. Move compensation to market rates. Remove personal costs from the business. Establish the monthly close process. Commission the first reviewed financial statements. Build the management reporting package that tracks the five operational metrics most relevant to the company's competitive performance.

Address the revenue quality agenda. Identify the ten accounts that represent the greatest concentration risk. Begin the systematic process of converting the key customer relationships from personal founder management to institutional account management. Start the contractual conversation with the customers who are currently buying on a purchase-order basis.

Years Three and Four: Build the Track Record

The third and fourth years are about generating the trailing performance that buyers will use as the basis of their valuation. The organizational changes made in years one and two begin producing financial results that are visible in the income statement. The normalized EBITDA and the reported EBITDA converge. The management team begins generating a track record of independent performance.

This is the period in which the strategic work that the bandwidth audit freed capacity for begins producing competitive advantage improvements. New customer wins that reduce concentration. Pricing improvements that expand margin. Operational efficiency initiatives that improve ROIC. Each of these improvements, accumulated over two years of consistent execution, contributes to the performance trajectory that a buyer will pay a premium to acquire.

Commission the preliminary valuation. Not to set a price expectation, but to identify the remaining gaps between the current position and the optimal transaction readiness profile. The preliminary valuation, conducted by an experienced M&A advisor with direct knowledge of the relevant transaction market, will surface the specific elements that require additional work before the transaction process begins. Two years is enough time to address almost anything the preliminary valuation identifies.

Year Five: Build the Narrative

The fifth year, the year before the transaction is intended to begin, is about converting the work of the previous four years into a coherent, defensible buyer narrative. Not a pitch. A narrative.

The distinction matters. A pitch is the seller's best case. A narrative is the factual story of what the company is, why it performs the way it does, and why a sophisticated buyer can be confident that the performance will continue. A pitch invites skepticism. A narrative invites confidence. The companies that achieve the best outcomes from a sale process are the ones whose management presentations feel like a description of documented reality, not an argument for a favorable interpretation of ambiguous facts.

Commission the internal quality of earnings analysis. Build the normalized EBITDA bridge, the documented reconciliation between reported and normalized earnings, before the buyer's team asks for it. Prepare the management team for the diligence interview process. The buyer's assessment of the management team will be formed as much by the quality of the diligence conversations as by the financial results.

The best sale processes describe documented reality. The rest argue for favorable interpretations.

The Conversation Most Founders Have Too Late

In my work as an operating advisor, I have the exit preparation conversation with founders at every stage of business development. The ones who have it earliest are, without exception, the ones who achieve the best outcomes. Not because they become less committed to their companies, quite the opposite. The discipline of preparing a company for a buyer's scrutiny is indistinguishable from the discipline of running a genuinely excellent company. The same practices that impress a sophisticated acquiror are the ones that produce a better run, higher margin, more resilient business in the present.

The conversation I wish more founders had earlier is a simple one. It begins with one question: if a sophisticated buyer evaluated your company today, not your financial presentation, but your actual business, what would they find that you would find uncomfortable to explain?

The honest answer to that question is the exit preparation agenda. It identifies, specifically, the elements of the business that are not yet ready for the level of scrutiny a serious transaction process will bring. It is not a comfortable conversation. It is also the most valuable one a founder can have, at the greatest possible distance from the transaction.

I have seen founders who had this conversation five years before their intended exit and used it as a management compass for everything they built in those five years. I have seen founders who had this conversation five months before their intended exit and spent those five months managing disappointment rather than managing value creation. The difference in outcomes between those two groups is not marginal. It is defining.

The founders who achieve the best exits are not the luckiest. They are not the ones who happened to have the most attractive businesses in the most favorable market conditions. They are the ones who understood, with enough lead time to act on the understanding, that a business prepared for the way buyers actually evaluate it is worth materially more than a business that is merely available for sale.

That preparation is available to every founder. It requires a willingness to be honest about the current state of the business, a willingness to invest in the disciplines that improve it, and, above all, a willingness to begin before the urgency of the transaction makes beginning feel necessary.

By then, it is too late to do it well.

Summary

The acquiror's perspective matters long before any transaction begins because it is one of the most honest evaluations a business will ever receive. Buyers look at management depth, revenue quality, margin durability, capital structure, and strategic coherence without any emotional investment in the narrative management prefers.

The five elements described in this chapter are not transaction only criteria. They are enduring indicators of business quality that management should be reviewing with the same rigor a buyer eventually will. A company that learns to see itself through the acquiror's lens before a buyer enters the process can address what it finds on its own terms.

One of the first and most consequential gaps that lens reveals is the distance between reported earnings and the business's true recurring earnings power. That gap, and what it costs when left unaddressed, is the focus of the next chapter.

12

THE MARGIN LEAK YOU ARE FUNDING WITHOUT KNOWING IT

THE GAP BETWEEN REPORTED PROFIT AND REAL EARNINGS: INVESTORS SEE IT FIRST, OWNERS SEE IT LAST.

I have been on the investing side of enough acquisition conversations to have watched the same moment unfold in different conference rooms, in different industries, with different owners. The owner arrives with a financial summary showing solid EBITDA from a business built over 15 or 20 years. The accountant has discussed a valuation multiple. The banker has said the market is supportive. The owner believes, reasonably and sincerely, that he understands what the company is worth.

The conversation that follows is rarely comfortable. Not because the business is weak. In most cases it is a genuinely good business. The discomfort comes from the fact that the earnings the owner has been living with and the earnings an investor or buyer is willing to underwrite are often not the same number. That gap is not fraud. It is not sloppy bookkeeping. It is the natural byproduct of how owner managed businesses are legitimately run, and it can materially change what outside capital is prepared to pay.

I call that gap the margin leak. It exists in almost every mid-sized private company I have evaluated as an investor and in every company I have advised ahead of a capital raise or sale. It is not a sign that the owner lacks financial sophistication. It is the predictable result of running a business in a way that optimizes for the owner's personal economics rather than for the earnings quality that lenders, investors, and acquirors require.

The margin leak matters most at a particular point in an owner's life. It matters when the company is strong enough to raise growth capital, refinance debt on better terms, or pursue a liquidity event. And it matters when the difference between reported earnings and investable earnings starts to determine the valuation, the structure, and the tone of the conversation.

This chapter is about that difference, where it comes from, how large it often is, and what an owner who is two to three years from a capital event should do now, before the investor or buyer identifies it first.

Buyers don't discover margin leaks. They reveal them — after pricing them in. Whoever finds the leak first owns the negotiation.

What Investors See in Your Financials That You Have Stopped Seeing

When an investor or sophisticated buyer evaluates a mid-sized company, the first step is usually reconstruction. That is not because the owner or the accountant is untrustworthy. It is because private company financial statements are built, entirely reasonably, around tax efficiency and owner benefit. They are rarely built to present the company's pure operating economics to an outside capital provider.

The reconstruction process, often formalized as a quality of earnings analysis, strips the company down to the economics a new owner would actually inherit. The question is not what this owner has chosen to run through the business. The question is what earnings the business would generate for a market rate management team operating the company without the current owner's personal cost structure, related party arrangements, or timing choices.

In practice that means identifying expenses a new owner would not incur; reclassifying items that are described as one time but recur often enough to be structural; normalizing revenue recognition so that each period reflects the economics of that period; and rebuilding EBITDA on a basis an investor can actually underwrite.

For a typical private company generating $4 million of reported EBITDA, the normalized figure can end up 15 to 40 percent higher or lower depending on the owner's practices and the reporting discipline of the business. That spread is not trivial. At a five times multiple, a swing of $800,000 in EBITDA means $4 million of enterprise value. At a six times multiple it is even more consequential.

The quality of earnings analysis that a buyer commissions may take three or four weeks and cost meaningful money. For the owner who has never done the work themselves, those weeks are when the basis of the conversation shifts from the number they expected to the number the buyer is actually willing to fund.

The Five Most Common Sources of the Margin Leak

1. Owner and family compensation above market

In many owner managed companies the owner's salary, bonus, benefits, and related family payroll are set to reflect the owner's total financial return from the company, not the market rate for the operating roles being performed. That is entirely legitimate from the owner's perspective. It does not reflect what a buyer's management team would cost. In a $30 million revenue company, the gap between actual compensation and market rate can easily reach $300,000 to $600,000 per year, which translates to $1.5 million to $3 million of enterprise value at a five times multiple.

2. Personal expenses running through the business

Vehicles, travel, entertainment, memberships, personal technology, advisory fees, and other lifestyle related costs often flow through a private company in ways that may be tax efficient and defensible, but that would not survive as true operating expenses under outside ownership. A buyer is not debating tax treatment. They are asking what portion of the cost structure would disappear if a professional management team replaced the founder. On a well run $30 million revenue company, this category alone can range from $150,000 to $400,000 annually, and in less disciplined situations it can be materially higher.

3. Above market related party arrangements

Leases from owner controlled real estate entities, service contracts with family affiliated businesses, and other related party arrangements are common in private companies. They are also one of the fastest ways value leaks out of the operating entity. If the facility rent, service fee, or supply arrangement is priced above market, the business's EBITDA is lower than it would be under arm's length economics. In a mid-sized company, this can mean $200,000 to $800,000 of annual cost and a much larger effect on valuation.

4. Items labeled non recurring that are actually recurring

Private company financials often contain charges described as one time that recur with surprising regularity when three years of history are reviewed together. Legal spend in litigious sectors, system upgrades every few years, periodic severance, and recurring repair projects are common examples. Each event may feel isolated in the year it occurs. Over time they describe the economic reality of the business. If a buyer concludes that these expenses are part of the recurring cost base, EBITDA is adjusted downward accordingly.

5. Revenue recognition inconsistency

Revenue timing is another common source of distortion. In many private companies revenue is recorded when invoiced, when cash is received, or according to habits that changed across periods rather than through a rigorously documented, consistently applied policy. The issue is not simply total revenue over several years. It is the quality, comparability, and predictability of earnings within each period. A buyer looking at irregular timing sees not just a possible adjustment but also weaker financial reporting quality, which can influence the multiple as much as the adjustment itself.

The Compounding Mathematics of the Margin Leak

The individual components of the leak can look manageable in isolation. Together they become economically significant very quickly.

Consider a company with $30 million in revenue and $4 million of reported EBITDA, roughly a 13 percent EBITDA margin. The owner has been told the business may be worth about $20 million at a five times multiple. Once the financials are normalized, the picture often changes dramatically.

Margin leak source	Annual amount	Valuation effect at 5x
Owner compensation above market	$350,000	$1,750,000
Personal expenses through the business	$280,000	$1,400,000
Above market related party lease	$220,000	$1,100,000
Recurring items labeled one time	$180,000	$900,000
Revenue timing adjustment	($150,000)	($750,000)
Total normalized EBITDA adjustment	$880,000 net	$4,400,000
Reported EBITDA	$4,000,000	$20,000,000
Normalized EBITDA	$4,880,000	$24,400,000

The normalized EBITDA in this illustration is $4.88 million, more than 20 percent above the reported figure. At a five times multiple, that is a $4.4 million difference in enterprise value before the conversation about the multiple itself even begins.

And that is only half the effect. A buyer who finds these issues late in diligence rarely applies the same multiple to the reconstructed earnings base. The leak itself sends a signal about financial discipline, reporting quality, and the possibility of additional adjustments still hidden in the statements. The result is often a discounted multiple on a lower starting figure. The prepared company earns a full multiple on normalized EBITDA. The unprepared company may receive a reduced multiple on reported EBITDA. That spread routinely creates a value gap of $4 million to $8 million in a company of this size.

Why This Matters Before the Exit

In a growth equity raise

A minority investor will rebuild earnings the same way an acquiror does. The normalized EBITDA becomes the pre money valuation anchor that determines how much ownership the investor receives for their capital. If the owner has not found and addressed the leak before the raise, they are often giving up more equity than the business's true economics require.

In a debt refinancing

Lenders and private credit funds size debt and set covenants against EBITDA. A business with $4.9 million of supportable EBITDA can borrow more, often at better terms, than one presenting only $4 million. A documented bridge from reported to normalized EBITDA can materially change both borrowing capacity and the quality of the banking conversation.

In exit preparation

The most valuable instruction I give owners who are within three years of a sale is simple: perform your own quality of earnings review before anyone else does. Not six months before the process begins. Ideally three years before. Three years of clean reporting, market rate compensation, and normalized arrangements create a financial history a buyer can trust. Six months of cleanup looks like presentation. Three years looks like reality.

The Self Diagnostic Protocol

1. Pull three years of detailed profit and loss data

Do not rely on a summary statement. Pull the full general ledger detail for the last three fiscal years and review expense categories line by line. Look for categories growing faster than revenue, categories materially above industry norms, and categories you would struggle to explain cleanly to an outside party.

2. List every commercial relationship with a related party

Write down every arrangement between the operating company and any entity in which you, a family member, or a close associate has a financial interest. For each one, document the annual dollars, the market rate, and the difference. That difference is value currently leaving the operating company.

3. Benchmark compensation to the market

Obtain current market data for the role you actually perform in the company and for each family member or associate on the payroll. Compare total cash compensation to those benchmarks. The excess above market is not necessarily wrong. It is simply an earnings adjustment waiting to happen.

4. Review three years of so called non recurring items

Compile every item classified as one time, extraordinary, or non recurring in the last three years. Ask whether a similar item appeared in another period, whether the underlying condition is likely to recur, and whether a buyer would really exclude it from ongoing earnings. Reclassify honestly.

5. Build the EBITDA bridge

Create a written reconciliation from reported EBITDA to normalized EBITDA, line by line, with a dollar amount and rationale for each adjustment. This bridge is one of the most valuable documents you can produce before a capital event. It tells an investor that you understand how capital evaluates your business, that you have already done the work, and that there are no surprises waiting to be discovered on their side of the table.

What the Owner Who Acts on This Discovers

Owners who complete this process almost always learn that their normalized EBITDA is meaningfully higher than the figure currently visible in their financial statements. That is good news. It means the company is more valuable than the reported numbers suggest. But value becomes visible to outside capital only when the business is run in a way that allows that value to be demonstrated cleanly.

In practical terms this means paying the owner a market rate and taking the excess through distributions rather than through operating expense lines. It means removing personal spending from the profit and loss statement or documenting it in a way that is transparent and objectively reviewable. It means rewriting or eliminating related party arrangements that do not reflect market pricing. It means tightening the monthly close, moving to reviewed financials, and documenting revenue recognition in a way that survives scrutiny.

None of this is conceptually difficult. All of it takes time. That is why the right runway is measured in years, not months. Three years of normalized reporting create a track record. Six months of cleanup create an argument. Buyers pay more for the track record.

The owners who do this work early describe a very different capital event from the one they had feared. The investor or buyer arrives having reviewed a bridge that confirms the economics rather than revises them. Diligence moves faster. The tone is less adversarial. The late stage price chip conversation either shrinks materially or never occurs at all. The business receives a valuation much closer to its actual economic value.

The owner who finds the margin leak three years before a capital event turns it into enterprise value. The owner who finds it three weeks before turns it into a negotiating disadvantage. The math is the same. The timing is what changes the outcome.

Summary

The margin leak described here is not evidence of a weak business. It is the predictable result of financial management choices that make complete sense inside a privately held company and create a very different picture once an outside investor reconstructs the earnings.

The five leak sources rarely look dramatic in isolation. Taken together, and then multiplied by the transaction multiple, they become one of the largest avoidable transfers of value in a mid-sized company sale or recapitalization. The self diagnostic protocol in this chapter is a way for the owner to find the leak before the buyer's diligence team does. But margin quality is only one dimension of what a buyer evaluates.

Once the numbers are normalized, the next question becomes whether the management team behind those numbers is genuinely portable, or whether the business still only makes full sense with the founder in the building. That is where the next chapter begins.

13

The Management Team a Buyer Pays For Is Not the One You Think You Have

The team that built this era can't run the next one. Here's how to build one that can.

There is a question I ask in every management presentation that a founding CEO gives me about their company, and it is never the question they expect.

The presentations are usually strong and the growth story is compelling. The market opportunity is real and the competitive differentiation is articulately described. The CEO knows the business with the intimacy of someone who has built it year by year, decision by decision, relationship by relationship. He can describe every major customer by name, every key supplier arrangement, every competitive threat and how he is thinking about it.

After the presentation concludes, after the questions about market size and revenue trajectory and capital efficiency have been asked and answered, I ask the one that determines more about the company's investable quality than any number in the deck. I ask the CEO to tell me, for each of the three or four most critical functions in the business, what would happen to that function's performance if the person currently running it were unexpectedly unavailable for the next ninety days.

The answers are almost always the same. Sales would be fine for the first month, then would start declining. Operations would hold for 60 days, then some things would start falling apart. The CEO himself would cover what he could. A couple of the customer relationships would need personal attention. The business would survive, but it would not be the same business that the presentation described.

That answer tells me the most important thing about the business that the presentation did not: the team I am being asked to invest in is not the team that will run the company after an investment or an ownership transition. The team I am looking at is a team built around one person's presence, judgment, and relationships. That person, by definition, is changing their role in whatever transaction we are discussing.

I am not describing a poorly managed company. The businesses that produce this answer are, in most cases, genuinely well run. The founder has been an exceptional CEO. The company has grown because of his talent, his energy, and his judgment. The problem is not what he built. The problem is that what he built is difficult to distinguish from who built it. And that distinction, between a business and its founder, is the distinction that determines whether the company can grow beyond him, attract the outside capital it needs, and achieve the valuation it deserves.

The team that got you to $40 million is rarely the team that gets you to $100 million. Different journey, different capabilities.

The Two Teams: Why Building Is Not the Same as Scaling

When I look back at the companies I have run and the investments I have made, one of the most consistent patterns I observe is this: the qualities that make someone exceptional at building a company from the ground up are specifically different from the qualities that make someone exceptional at scaling a company past a certain threshold of complexity and organizational size.

The builder, the person who is most valuable in the early and middle stages of a company's development, thrives in conditions of ambiguity. He operates in an environment of resource constraint, and proximity to every significant decision. He is comfortable wearing multiple hats. He makes decisions quickly because he has to, and he is often right because his direct proximity to every part of the business gives him information that no organizational system could produce as efficiently. His value is in doing, and often in doing everything that matters personally.

The scaler, the person most valuable when a company reaches the organizational complexity of 20 million dollars in revenue and above, thrives in conditions of defined accountabilit with process discipline and organizational design. He builds systems rather than doing things directly, and hires specialists rather than generalists. He measures outcomes rather than managing activities. His value is in creating organizational capability that functions independently of his personal involvement.

Most mid-sized companies have management teams that are composed entirely of builders, people recruited and developed during the building phase who are deeply loyal to the company and its founder They are deeply knowledgeable about the company's history and culture, and deeply unequipped for the specific organizational demands of the scaling phase. They are not the wrong people for the company that existed. They are the wrong people for the company that needs to exist.

The founder who recognizes this distinction early enough, who understands that the transition from building to scaling requires a fundamental change in the talent architecture, not just an upgrade in the same direction, is the founder who can manage the transition without the cultural rupture and organizational trauma that an abrupt talent replacement produces. The founder who recognizes it only when it forces itself into his awareness, through a failed growth initiative, a missed acquisition integration, or a capital event that underperforms expectations because the management depth is not there, has a harder problem to solve with less time to solve it.

The Outside Talent Problem: Why mid-sized Companies Struggle to Import What They Need

I want to address something that founders rarely discuss with the honesty it deserves. It touches on personal identity, organizational loyalty, and the complicated feelings that accompany the recognition that the team you built. The team that was there during the hard years, may not be the team that takes the company where you want it to go.

Most founders know, at some level, that they need to bring in outside talent to support the next phase of growth. The knowledge is not the problem. The problem is that importing talent from outside into a mid-sized company that has been built around an internal culture, a set of internal relationships, and a management style defined by one person's personality is one of the most consistently difficult organizational challenges in business. And most founders underestimate that difficulty with remarkable consistency.

The outside hire arrives with capabilities the company needs. He has scaled a comparable function at a larger company, and has managed teams of the size the company is trying to build toward. He has implemented the systems, the processes, and the organizational disciplines that the company currently lacks. On paper, he is exactly what is required.

He is also, in the first six to 12 months, an organizational foreign body. The internal team, which has been operating on an implicit set of norms, relationships, and expectations that have accumulated over years, experiences him as a disruption. The founder, who managed his existing team through personal relationship and institutional knowledge, now manages a team that has a member he does not have the same relationship with. The outside hire, who succeeded in a previous organization by applying his expertise directly, discovers that his expertise is only half of what he needs. The other half is the organizational legitimacy to apply it, and that legitimacy must be earned in a culture that did not invite him, has no template for people like him, and has no particular reason to grant it quickly.

Outside hires rarely fail on capability. They fail on conditions the organization never built.

I have watched this failure pattern play out too many times to regard it as exceptional. A founder identifies a capability gap, recruits aggressively for the specific skills required. He makes what he believes is an excellent hire, and then watches in frustration as the new executive fails to produce the outcomes that justified the hire. The founder's conclusion is typically that the hiring process failed, that the wrong person was selected. In most cases, that is not the accurate diagnosis. The right person was hired into the wrong conditions.

Understanding what those conditions are, and how to create them, is the most important talent management skill available to a mid-sized company founder who is trying to build the organizational depth that growth and value creation both require.

The Six Questions That Reveal Management Team Transferability

Before addressing how to build the management depth the company needs, it is worth being precise about what the management depth assessment actually measures. This is not a performance evaluation. The question is not whether the management team performs well under current conditions. It is whether the management team's performance is transferable, whether it will continue if the conditions that currently support it change.

The following six questions, applied honestly to each member of the senior team, produce the most accurate picture of management transferability I have found. They are the same questions a sophisticated investor or buyer applies in their management assessment, usually more rigorously and more dispassionately than a founder can apply to people he has worked alongside for years.

Question 1, The Replacement Test

The question: If this person were replaced tomorrow with someone of equivalent general management experience who had not previously worked in this company, how long would it take for the function they lead to return to its current performance level? Within 90 days?

✔ If the answer is yes: The function's performance is embedded in systems, processes, and documented practices that a capable successor can learn and apply within 90 days. The executive is leading a function, not embodying one.

✖ If the answer is no: The answer is longer than six months, or you genuinely cannot answer it because the function's performance depends on this person's specific relationships, tacit knowledge, or working style that cannot be transferred. The function is person dependent, not system embedded.

Question 2, The Autonomy Test

The question: Does this executive make the most important decisions in their domain independently, without consulting the CEO first, without seeking informal approval, and without the CEO's involvement being a normal part of the decision process?

✔ If the answer is yes: The executive owns their domain. Decisions that should be made at their level are made at their level. The CEO is informed, not consulted. The function operates with genuine independent authority.

✖ If the answer is no: The most important decisions in this domain routinely involve the CEO in a way that goes beyond governance oversight into operational or management. The executive is executing the CEO's judgment rather than exercising their own. When the CEO is unavailable, important decisions in this domain either wait or are made at lower quality.

Question 3, The Documentation Test

The question: If every process, decision framework, and operational practice that this executive uses in their daily management of the function were written down and given to a capable successor, would that documentation be sufficient to maintain the function's performance?

✔ If the answer is yes: The practices that produce results in this function are explicit, documented, and transmissible. They live in the organizational system rather than in the executive's head. Knowledge transfer is possible because the knowledge has been made transferable.

✘ If the answer is no: The most important practices in this function are tacit. They exist in the executive's judgment, intuition, and experience but have never been made explicit. A capable successor would need six to eighteen months of direct observation and mentorship to understand how the function actually works at the level that produces its current results.

Question 4, The Relationship Test

The question: Are the most important external relationships that support this function, key customers, key suppliers, key partners, relationships with the company or relationships with the individual?

✔ If the answer is yes: The relationships are institutional. They are managed through formal account management structures They are documented through CRM systems, and would survive a change in the executive who manages them with minimal disruption to the commercial relationship.

✘ If the answer is no: The relationships are personal. The key customer calls this executive's mobile phone. The key supplier negotiation happens over golf. The key partnership is held together by a personal trust that has accumulated over years of direct relationship management. These relationships are genuinely valuable, and genuinely non transferable in their current form.

Question 5, The Succession Test

The question: Is there an identified successor for this executive, someone in the organization who is actively being developed for the role, who understands the function's strategy and operational requirements, and who could step into the role within six months with adequate support?

✔ If the answer is yes: The function has a defined succession path. The successor is known, is actively developing the required capabilities, and has been explicitly told that they are being prepared for this responsibility. Management depth is being built deliberately.

✖ If the answer is no: There is no identified internal successor. If asked, the honest answer is that the organization does not currently have someone ready to step into this role. The function is a single point of failure. A departure, a health event, or an ownership transition would create an immediate capability crisis.

Question 6, The Scale Test

The question: Is this executive capable of leading this function at twice the company's current scale, with twice the team size and the operational complexity, and twice the organizational demands? Has he led at that scale before, and is there evidence that he can?

✔ If the answer is yes: The executive has operated at greater scale than the company currently requires, he is not at his capability ceiling. The company's next growth phase can be led by the team currently in place, and the team's track record at comparable scale provides evidence for that assessment.

✖ If the answer is no: The executive has been excellent at the current scale but has not managed at the scale the company's next phase requires. He may grow into it, or he may not. The uncertainty about whether the current team can lead the next phase is a genuine risk that an investor or buyer will price into their assessment.

Importing Outside Talent: The Conditions That Determine Success or Failure

The management transferability assessment almost always produces the same finding: one to three functions have high founder dependency, insufficient documentation, and no clear succession path. The appropriate response is to bring in outside talent with the specific capabilities required to lead those functions to the company's next level. And this is where most mid-sized companies make the same series of mistakes in the same sequence.

Mistake 1: Hiring for Skills Without Diagnosing the Cultural Fit Requirement

The mid-sized company that has been built around a founder's personality has a culture with specific and often invisible rules: how decisions are made, how disagreement is expressed, how relationships with the founding team are navigated, what kinds of behavior are rewarded and what kinds create friction. An outside hire who is not assessed against these cultural requirements, not just the skills requirements, will have a specific kind of failure even when the skills are precisely right.

The most common version of this failure is the executive who brings corporate process and institutional discipline into a culture that has operated on entrepreneurial instinct and personal relationship. The corporate executive introduces governance frameworks, reporting requirements, and organizational structures that are entirely appropriate for a company of the current size. The existing team experiences this as bureaucratic, impersonal, and disrespectful of the way things have always worked. The outside hire is not wrong. The culture is not wrong. They are incompatible, and nobody checked before the offer was made.

Mistake 2: Insufficient Onboarding Investment for an Adequate Time Period

The standard onboarding period for a senior outside hire in a mid-sized company is approximately 60 to 90 days of structured orientation, followed by an expectation that the executive is performing independently. This timeline is adequate for a company with a well documented culture. There are clear processes, and an established management team that actively supports the integration. It is entirely inadequate for a founder led company where the implicit rules are numerous, the internal relationships are complex, and the existing team has no template for how to work with someone who joined from outside.

I recommend a 12 month structured integration for any senior outside hire into a mid-sized company that has been founder led for more than five years. Not 12 months of orientation but 12 months of explicit attention to the integration, including monthly check ins between the CEO. The new executive would focus specifically on the integration experience with a formal assignment of an internal integration partner from the existing senior team. There should be explicit permission for the outside hire to surface integration friction without fear of it being interpreted as performance failure.

Mistake 3: Unclear Authority and Undercut Decisions

The founder who brings in an outside executive to lead a function and then continues to be the de facto decision maker in that function has not brought in outside talent. He has brought in a very expensive middle manager. The management team will read the founder's continued operational involvement as a signal that the outside executive does not actually have authority, and they will be correct.

The transition of genuine decision making authority to an outside hire is among the most difficult things a founder can do, because it requires accepting that the outside hire will make decisions differently than the founder would have, and that this is acceptable. Some of those decisions will be better. Some will be worse. The founder who cannot tolerate a different decision making approach in a function that is no longer his primary responsibility has not made a hire. He has made a casting decision in a performance where he intends to remain the lead.

> ***The team watched the founder override the new hire three times and drew the correct conclusion: he doesn't actually run this function. After that, the hire has failed — whatever the payroll says.***

Five Practices That Build Genuine Management Depth

The following practices address both the assessment and the development challenge: building the management team that can lead the company's next growth phase, recruiting the outside talent that the internal team cannot provide, and creating the organizational conditions in which outside talent can be successfully integrated. They are presented in the sequence in which they should be applied.

Practice 1, Conduct the Transferability Assessment Before You Need the Results

Apply the six assessment questions to every member of the senior team at least 18 months before any contemplated capital event, growth initiative, or strategic transition that will require the team to perform at a materially higher level. The assessment is most valuable when it is conducted without the urgency of an immediate need, because urgency compresses the options. An honest transferability assessment 18 months in advance produces a talent development agenda with adequate time to execute. The same assessment conducted six months before a transaction produces a talent emergency with insufficient time to resolve.

Practice 2, Distinguish Between the Team You Have And the Team You Need

The transferability assessment will reveal a specific gap between the management team that currently exists and the management team required for the company's next phase. That gap has two components: the functions that are currently founder dependent and need to be institutionalized; and the functions that need capabilities beyond what the current team can develop within the required timeframe. The first component is addressed through internal development and documentation. The second component requires an outside hire. Mixing these two responses, trying to develop internally what needs to be hired externally, or hiring externally for functions that an internal candidate could reach with structured support, is the most common talent strategy error in mid-sized company growth management.

Practice 3, Hire The Outside Talent For Where You Are Going, Not Where You Are

The outside hire should have already led the function you are asking him to build at a company of the size you intend to be in three years, not the size you are today. An executive who has managed a 30 person sales team at a company generating 80 million dollars in revenue brings something that an executive who has managed a 15 person sales team at a 30 million dollar company does not bring: the specific organizational experience of scale. He has encountered the management challenges that come with the next level before he encounters them in your company. That experience is not available from internal development and cannot be purchased from a smaller external candidate at a lower cost. The additional cost of a genuinely experienced outside hire is the least expensive form of insurance available against the management failure of a growth initiative.

Practice 4, Structure the Integration As A Twelve Month Program, Not A Sixty Day Orientation

Build a formal 12 month integration program for every outside hire above the director level. The program includes: a 90 day listening tour in which the new executive observes, asks questions, and builds relationships before implementing significant changes; an explicit integration partner from the existing senior team whose role is to provide organizational context, identify friction early, and advocate for the integration in the internal culture; monthly CEO check ins focused exclusively on the integration experience, not the functional performance metrics; a clear articulation of the authority the new executive has, the decisions he owns, and the decisions that require CEO involvement; and a twelve month review that assesses the integration quality alongside the performance results. The twelve month investment in structured integration produces significantly higher retention, faster productivity, and better cultural absorption than the sixty day standard.

Practice 5, Transfer Authority Explicitly, Publicly, And Without Retrieval

The day an outside executive begins leading a function, the founder's relationship with that function changes. This change must be explicit, public, and irreversible, at least within the ninety day foundation period. Explicit: the founder tells the management team directly which decisions now belong to the new executive and which decisions remain at the CEO level. Public: the founder demonstrates the transfer by visibly deferring to the new executive in management meetings when his domain is discussed, even when the founder's instinct is to answer. Without retrieval: when the new executive makes a decision the founder would have made differently, the founder does not override it except in cases of clear material harm. The management team will test the authority transfer through observation. The first three or four decisions the new executive makes will be watched carefully by the entire internal team to determine whether the transfer is real. If the founder retrieves the decision each time, the transfer was theater. If he allows the decisions to stand, the transfer begins to become real.

What Genuine Management Depth Produces, Beyond the Investor Conversation

I want to be clear about something that often gets lost in the transaction preparation framing of management depth: the organizational capability described in this article is not primarily valuable because it impresses investors and buyers. It is primarily valuable because it makes the company a better, faster growing, more resilient business in the present.

A company with genuine management depth, where the most critical functions are led by people who can perform independently of the founder, who have already managed at the scale the company is targeting, and whose performance is embedded in organizational systems rather than in personal relationships and tacit knowledge, is a company that can execute its strategic agenda at a pace and quality that a founder dependent organization cannot match.

It can pursue multiple strategic initiatives simultaneously because the management bandwidth to execute them is genuinely distributed across the leadership team. It can absorb the departure of a key executive without the organizational crisis that a single point of failure team produces. It can integrate an acquisition because the operational leaders can manage the complexity of integration alongside the complexity of the existing business. It can pursue a capital raise or a sale process without the CEO spending 90 percent of his management time on the transaction, because the business can be run at a high level by the team while the transaction consumes his attention.

These capabilities are worth more to the company on the day they are built than they are at the exit. The exit is when they are monetized. They are built through the daily discipline of recruiting for scale, integrating with intention, and transferring authority with conviction.

I have had the conversation about management team transferability with founders at every stage of growth and at every stage of investment readiness. The founders who act on the assessment early, who build the outside talent and the organizational depth before they need it for a transaction, uniformly describe the same experience. The company grows faster. The founder's daily experience of running the company improves materially, because he is no longer the last line of defense on every significant decision. And when the capital event eventually occurs, the management team conversation with investors is not a negotiation about risk. It is a demonstration of capability.

That demonstration, of a management team that performs at a level genuinely independent of the founder's presence, is worth more in a transaction valuation than almost any other single characteristic of a mid-sized private company. It commands a premium multiple. It compresses the diligence timeline. It eliminates the earnout requirement that founders despise and investors impose specifically because management risk is unresolved.

Build a team that makes investors ask about its next chapter — not about how long you'll have to stay.

The Honest Conversation the Founder Needs to Have With Himself

I want to close with something that is rarely said directly in the management advice literature but that is, in my experience, the most important factor in whether a founder successfully builds the management depth the company requires.

The management team transferability problem is ultimately a founder identity problem. A founder who has been the center of organizational decision making for 10 to15 years has a self concept that is deeply intertwined with being the person who knows the most, decides the most, and is the most needed. Building a genuinely capable outside team, a team that can lead the company at the next level without requiring the founder's involvement in every significant matter, requires the founder to let go of the specific elements of that identity that are incompatible with a scalable organization.

He must let go of being the smartest person in every room in his company. A genuinely capable outside executive, recruited because he has already done what the company is trying to do, will know more than the founder about her domain. That is the point. It should feel like relief. For many founders, it initially feels like a threat.

He must let go of the relationships that are personally his but organizationally the company's. The key customer who calls his mobile phone needs to be transitioned, over time and with the founder's active facilitation, to a relationship with the institution rather than the individual. This is uncomfortable because those relationships are genuinely valuable and genuinely personal. It is also necessary, because an institutional asset that lives on a single person's mobile phone is not an institutional asset.

He must let go of the performance standard that says his way of doing something is the right way. An outside executive with comparable experience will do things differently, and will sometimes be right to do so. The founder who can observe this with curiosity rather than judgment is the founder who retains the outside talent he recruits. The founder who corrects every deviation from his preferred approach is the founder who produces the outside hire failure pattern I described earlier.

None of this is comfortable. All of it is available to a founder who understands that his most important job, at the stage of the company's development where outside talent and management depth become essential, is to build something that is stronger than his own ability to be present for it. The company that outlasts the founder's central involvement is not a smaller version of what he built. It is the full expression of what he was building toward all along.

Build a team that doesn't need you, and you haven't become irrelevant. You've become investable, valuable, and free.

Summary

The management transferability assessment in this chapter forces a founder to look at the team in a way most founders naturally resist. The question is not whether the team performs well in the current environment, where the founder is still present to compensate, coach, and decide. The question is whether the team can perform when the founder's role changes or disappears.

The six questions in the chapter reveal where authority is real, where knowledge is still tacit, and where relationships are personal rather than institutional. They also show why importing outside talent so often fails, not because the hire lacked capability, but because the organization never created the conditions under which that capability could be used.

Once that picture becomes clear, the buyer's perspective sharpens further. The next chapter steps fully to the other side of the table and shows what private equity finds when it examines the business and how it prices every unresolved issue it uncovers.

14

The Decision Your Organization Is Avoiding Is the One That Determines Your Outcome

THE DECISIONS WITH THE MOST WEIGHT ARE THE ONES ORGANIZATIONS AVOID MAKING PRECISELY BECAUSE OF THAT WEIGHT.

I have a question I have learned to ask in the first serious conversation with any new management team. Not in the opening meeting, that conversation is still too formal, the team too collectively composed, to produce the honest answer I am looking for. I ask it a few sessions in, when I have enough relational capital to make the question feel less threatening and the team has enough comfort with me to answer it truthfully.

The question is this: what is the most important decision this organization has been meaning to make for the past six months and has not made?

Every management team has an answer. In my experience across dozens of companies as CEO, chairman, investor, and advisor, I have never asked this question and received a blank response. The decision exists. The management team knows it exists. In most cases, every member of the team knows it exists independently, without coordination or conference. The deferred decision has not been missed. It has been observed, discussed in fragments, and collectively avoided.

What varies is the category of decision and the duration of the deferral. Sometimes the team describes a personnel decision: a senior executive whose performance has been inadequate for a year and who is being managed around rather than managed out. Sometimes it is a strategic decision: a business unit or product line that is clearly not contributing proportionally to the company's growth and that should be rationalized but has not been. Sometimes it is a customer decision: a relationship whose cost to serve exceeds its revenue contribution and whose persistence in the portfolio is limiting the resources available for better opportunities. Sometimes it is a capital decision: a financing arrangement that no longer reflects the company's credit quality but whose renegotiation has been repeatedly deprioritized.

In every case, the deferred decision shares a specific set of characteristics that distinguish it from the ordinary backlog of management work. It is not deferred because no one has thought about it. It is not deferred because the analysis is incomplete. It is deferred because making it requires something that the normal management process is specifically designed to avoid: a clear, explicit, public choice between two or more options whose consequences include making someone, or many people, uncomfortable.

Deferred decisions aren't failures of analysis. They're failures of nerve, and they compound weekly.

Why the Most Important Decisions Are the Most Avoided

The relationship between decision importance and decision avoidance is not a paradox. It is a mechanism. And understanding the mechanism is the prerequisite for addressing it.

The most important decisions a management team faces in the course of a year share a common structural characteristic: they require an explicit prioritization that, by definition, produces a winner and a loser. Deciding that Business Unit A will receive the incremental capital means Business Unit B will not. Deciding that a senior executive is not performing at the required level and must transition out means that executive's tenure is ending. Deciding to exit a customer relationship means the revenue associated with it disappears from the top line before the resources consumed by serving it are freed. Deciding to pursue one strategic direction means explicitly not pursuing the alternatives.

These are all genuinely difficult decisions, and the difficulty is not analytical. The analytical case is usually clear. The financial analysis of which business unit deserves the capital has been completed. The performance record of the underperforming executive is documented. The customer profitability analysis showing the negative contribution of the relationship is in the management reporting package. The strategic option assessment has been reviewed by the board.

The difficulty is relational and political. The leader of the underfunded business unit will be disappointed and possibly demoralized. The underperforming executive is a colleague who has been with the company through difficult years and whose departure will require acknowledgment of a management failure as much as a performance one. The unprofitable customer relationship involves a personal connection that predates the current strategic priorities. The rejected strategic alternative had a champion who advocated for it with genuine conviction.

Every force in the normal organizational environment pushes against making these decisions at the moment when making them would be most effective. The management calendar is always full of operational demands that are more immediate. The management meeting agenda is always controlled by the items that generate the least interpersonal friction. The social contract of the leadership team tilts consistently toward the consensus that preserves relationships rather than the decision that optimizes outcomes.

The most important decisions require admitting something isn't working. That's uncomfortable, and discomfort is the most reliable predictor of deferral.

What I Learned About This From the Chair

I want to describe a specific pattern I encountered repeatedly in my years as CEO and chairman, because it captures the organizational psychology of decision avoidance more precisely than any abstract description I can offer.

In every organization I led or oversaw at the board level, there was a version of the same phenomenon: a decision that the management team was clearly aware needed to be made, that was visible in every indicator the management reporting system produced, and that was consistently not made because the people with the authority and the information to make it also had the relationships and the organizational incentives that made making it uncomfortable.

The most common version was the performance decision about a senior team member. In virtually every company I have been involved with as a chairman or investor, there has been at least one member of the senior leadership team who was not performing at the level the company required, who had been in that state for longer than the situation warranted, and whose continued tenure was being rationalized through a set of explanations that had stopped being honest some time ago.

The explanations were always sympathetic and always partly true. The person had been with the company during a difficult period and their loyalty was real. There were personal circumstances that made the timing feel particularly unkind. The search for a replacement would take six months and the company could not afford the gap. The person was performing adequately in some dimensions even if not in the critical ones. Each of these explanations was an honest observation about a real consideration. None of them were the actual reason the decision was not being made. The actual reason was that making it was going to be painful for everyone involved, including the person making it.

What I learned, from watching this pattern play out in organization after organization, was that the duration of the deferral was almost perfectly correlated with the eventual cost of the decision. The performance problem that was addressed at three months was manageable. The same performance problem addressed at twelve months had typically produced a set of secondary consequences, team dynamics distorted around the person's limitations, customer relationships strained by underperformance, strategic initiatives stalled because the function was not executing, that made the resolution significantly more complex and more expensive. The longer the avoidance, the larger the problem that was eventually unavoidable.

This pattern holds not just for personnel decisions but for every category of consequential organizational decision. The deferred strategic choice costs more when it is finally made than it would have cost if it had been made earlier, because the alternatives have become less favorable, the resources that might have funded them have been consumed by the continued pursuit of the wrong direction, and the organizational energy that might have executed them has been dissipated by the confusion of having no clear priority.

Deferral doesn't change the analysis. It changes the options — fewer and more expensive with every month that passes.

The Five Categories of Avoided Decision in mid-sized Organizations

Decision avoidance is not random. It clusters around five specific categories of decision that share the same characteristics: high consequence, clear analytical case, and significant relational or political cost that makes the organizational dynamics of the decision more difficult than the analytical ones.

I have seen each of these categories in every organization I have worked with seriously. They are not aberrations. They are structural features of how organizations manage the tension between the need to make hard decisions and the social and political pressures that make those decisions difficult.

Avoidance Pattern 1, The Performance Decision That Has Been Reframed As A Development Challenge

Why it is avoided: Addressing a senior executive's sustained underperformance requires the management team to acknowledge that the hire was wrong, the management support was insufficient, or both. It requires a conversation that is difficult, a search process that is time consuming, and a transition that produces organizational uncertainty. All of these are real costs. The organization avoids them by reframing the performance problem as a development opportunity: more coaching, a revised role scope, additional support resources, a performance improvement process with a timeline that extends the deferral while appearing to address the problem.

The organizational signal: The management meeting that spends thirty minutes discussing how to better support an executive's development rather than fifteen minutes acknowledging that the role is not matched to the person's capabilities. The quarterly business review that documents underperformance in careful language while committing to a plan that implicitly accepts twelve more months of the same outcome. The board presentation that describes a 'transition underway' for a situation that has been underway for a year.

The compound cost of continued deferral: The cost of a deferred personnel decision is quadratic, not linear. Each month of continued underperformance produces direct cost through the function's reduced effectiveness, and compounding cost through the organizational behaviors that form around the performance gap: the workarounds that absorb management bandwidth, the team members who adjust their own performance expectations downward to match the visible standard, the strategic work that is not getting done because the function is not functioning.

Avoidance Pattern 2, The Business or Product Rationalization That Threatens a Champion

Why it is avoided: Every mid-sized company carries activities, business units, product lines, customer segments, geographic markets, that absorb organizational resources disproportionate to their strategic or financial contribution. The analysis showing the disproportion is usually available. The decision to rationalize is not made because every underperforming activity has a champion whose professional identity is attached to it, and whose cooperation is needed for the activities that are performing well. The rationalization is deferred indefinitely, disguised as a 'strategic review underway' or a 'turnaround plan in development.'

The organizational signal: The strategic planning session that reviews the portfolio against objective criteria and identifies the underperforming activities, and then produces a 'three year improvement plan' for each of them rather than a decision about which ones should continue. The resource allocation conversation that returns each year with the same distribution, adjusted at the margins for budget reasons, never reflecting the stark performance differentiation in the portfolio that the financial reporting shows.

The compound cost of continued deferral: Portfolio complexity consumes management attention in ways that go beyond the direct cost of supporting the underperforming activities. It distributes management bandwidth across a wider surface area than the strategic priorities require, prevents the focused investment in the highest opportunity activities that would produce compound competitive advantage, and signals to the organization that the management team is unwilling to make the choices that a real strategy requires.

Avoidance Pattern 3, The Customer Relationship That Is Being Retained Out of Personal History

Why it is avoided: Some customer relationships exist in the company's portfolio because they were essential at an earlier stage of the company's development and are maintained now because terminating them feels disloyal to the people and the history those relationships represent. The analysis shows the relationship is unprofitable on a fully loaded cost to serve basis, or that it consumes a service quality and management attention that the current business model cannot sustain for the economics it generates. The decision to restructure or exit the relationship is deferred because the relationship predates the strategic priorities that make it a poor fit.

The organizational signal: The customer who is on the books at a price negotiated five years ago when the company needed the volume, whose service requirements have grown with the business but whose willingness to pay has not. The 'legacy account' that appears in every pipeline review as a special case, handled directly by the CEO or a senior relationship holder because the normal account management process cannot absorb the demands at the current economics.

The compound cost of continued deferral: The opportunity cost of the deferred customer rationalization decision is specific and quantifiable: the management hours, service resources, and organizational attention consumed by the retained relationship are hours, resources, and attention unavailable to the relationships whose economics justify the investment. The company is not just carrying a bad relationship. It is paying for that relationship with the diminished capacity to serve the good ones.

Avoidance Pattern 4, The Strategic Pivot That Requires Admitting the Current Direction Is Wrong

Why it is avoided: The most consequential strategic decisions, the ones that change where a company is going rather than how fast it is going there, require the management team to acknowledge that the current direction is not producing the results it was expected to produce. This acknowledgment is politically and psychologically expensive: it implicitly criticizes the decision making that set the current direction, generates accountability for the resources consumed by that direction, and raises questions about the management team's judgment that no leader finds comfortable to invite.

The organizational signal: The company that has been building toward a market position for two years that has not materialized, but whose management team is producing increasingly detailed plans for achieving the original objective rather than reassessing whether the objective remains the right one. The strategic plan that is updated annually with revised timelines and improved methodology for the same directional commitment, with the same absence of honest evaluation of whether the direction itself was correct.

The compound cost of continued deferral: The organization that will not acknowledge a wrong strategic direction cannot correct it. The resources committed to the wrong direction continue flowing there. The competitive dynamics of the market continue shifting in ways that the company is not positioned to respond to. The most valuable thing about the wrong direction, the information that was generated by attempting it, is not converted into strategic learning because the organization has not admitted the attempt failed.

Avoidance Pattern 5, The Capital or Financial Decision Whose Cost Has Been Normalized

Why it is avoided: Some financial arrangements that are actively harmful to the company's performance have been in place long enough that the management team has stopped experiencing them as harmful. The high cost debt whose interest expense absorbs margin that should fund growth has been present long enough that it is treated as a fixed cost rather than a decision. The equity arrangement whose terms are no longer appropriate for the company's current scale has been in place long enough that its dilutive effects are accepted as permanent. The pricing structure that undervalues the company's contribution has been in place long enough that it feels like the market rate.

The organizational signal: The financial covenant that has been the subject of a 'waiver request' from the lender three times in as many years, with a management team that has learned to route operational decisions around the covenant rather than addressing the capital structure that makes the covenant a recurring constraint. The pricing conversation that was supposed to happen eighteen months ago and has been rescheduled to avoid the customer friction, with the original pricing still in place.

The compound cost of continued deferral: Financial arrangements that have been normalized lose their cost visibility in management reporting and management conversation. They become invisible constraints, present in every decision the company makes without being acknowledged in any of them. The company optimizes within the constraint rather than examining whether the constraint should exist at all.

The Deferred Decision Diagnostic: Finding What Your Organization Is Avoiding

The diagnostic I have found most effective for surfacing deferred decisions is not a systematic management process. It is a direct question, asked with enough relational permission to receive an honest answer, to the person in the room who is most likely to have independent visibility into the organization's most significant avoidances.

In a CEO role, that person is often a board member who has been around long enough to watch the same issues reappear in presentation after presentation without resolution. In a chairman role, it is often a senior member of the management team whose position gives them visibility across functions but whose organizational role does not require them to defend the decisions that are being avoided. In an advisory role, it is often the CEO herself, who knows what is being avoided better than anyone and whose ability to acknowledge it depends on whether the conversation feels safe enough to be honest.

Beyond the direct question, there are three specific diagnostic signals that I look for in management meetings, management reporting, and management conversation that reliably indicate the presence of a deferred decision of significant consequence.

Diagnostic Signal	What It Reveals
The same issue appears in three consecutive quarterly reviews without a decision or a deadline	The issue has been identified, analyzed, and discussed. It has not been decided. The recurrence without resolution is the signal that the analytical work is complete and the organizational will to decide is the constraint.
The management team produces more sophisticated analysis of a problem in each review cycle without changing the conclusion	Progressive sophistication of analysis without progress toward decision is the organizational equivalent of displacement activity: the effort feels productive and the output is impressive, but the fundamental avoidance is intact.
A topic that is discussed in one on one conversations is consistently absent from the full management meeting agenda	The informal network of the organization is processing a problem that the formal management structure is not. This gap between what is discussed privately and what is discussed officially identifies the topics whose political or relational cost makes them too expensive to raise in a structured setting.
The leader of a struggling area presents the most detailed and most positive updates at management meetings	The person with the most at risk from a decision being made often generates the most activity around that decision without moving it forward. The detailed update, the improved metric, the new initiative, each creates the appearance of progress while maintaining the deferral.
The management team agrees quickly and unanimously on any topic involving the deferred decision area	Quick consensus in a normally deliberative management team indicates that the group has learned not to open the subject. Speed of agreement is not the signal of alignment. It is the signal of collective avoidance.

The Political Economy of Decision Avoidance

I want to be specific about the organizational forces that produce and sustain decision avoidance, because naming them precisely is the prerequisite for addressing them. Vague exhortations to 'make the hard decisions' and 'hold people accountable' do not produce behavioral change in management teams. Understanding the specific mechanism that produces the avoidance is what enables the specific intervention that addresses it.

Decision avoidance in mid-sized companies is sustained by three interlocking organizational forces, each of which is individually rational and collectively corrosive.

The Social Insurance of Shared Deferral

When a consequential decision is not made, the responsibility for not making it is shared among everyone who participated in the management process that deferred it. No single person is accountable for the avoidance because the avoidance was a group product. This shared non accountability is the social insurance that makes deferral the path of least organizational resistance: the cost of not deciding is distributed across the team, while the cost of deciding, making the difficult conversation, managing the consequences, accepting responsibility for the outcome, is concentrated in the person who makes the call.

The executive who makes the deferred decision accepts individual responsibility for both the decision and its consequences. The executive who participates in the deferral shares collective non responsibility. Given this asymmetry, the rational individual choice in a management team with no external accountability mechanism is consistently to participate in the deferral and avoid the personal exposure of the decision.

The Optimism Bias in Forward Projection

Management teams consistently believe that deferred decisions will become easier to make in the future than they are today. The performance problem will become clearer with more time. The strategic direction will prove itself or fail more definitively. The customer relationship will restructure itself naturally. The financial arrangement will expire or improve with market conditions. Each of these beliefs is occasionally correct and almost always wrong as a basis for deferral strategy.

The organizational reality is the opposite: deferred decisions almost always become harder to make, not easier. The performance problem becomes more entrenched as the organization adapts around it. The strategic direction becomes more defended as more resources are committed to it. The customer relationship becomes more difficult to exit as more expectations are set around its continuation. The financial arrangement becomes more embedded as the company's operations adapt to its constraints. Time does not make hard decisions easier. It makes them more expensive.

The Measurement Absence for Non Decisions

Organizations measure what is done. They almost never measure what is not done. The financial reporting captures the results of the decisions that were made. It does not capture the opportunity cost of the decisions that were deferred. The performance review evaluates the executive's actions. It does not evaluate the decisions the executive avoided making that would have produced better outcomes.

In the absence of measurement, the non decision is invisible as a management failure. The management team sees the consequences of bad decisions, the failed product launch, the missed revenue target, the customer defection, and correctly attributes them to decisions that were made poorly. It does not see the consequences of the decisions not made, because those consequences accumulate as a gradual failure to reach potential rather than as an acute failure visible in the reporting.

Five Practices That Create an Organization That Decides

The solution to organizational decision avoidance is not to hire bolder executives or to create a culture that celebrates difficult decisions as a matter of identity. These approaches address the symptom rather than the mechanism. The mechanism is structural, it is produced by the specific incentive architecture, information architecture, and accountability architecture of the organization. The solution is structural as well.

Practice 1, The Deferred Decision Inventory

At the beginning of each quarter, the CEO or the most senior leader in the room asks every member of the management team to identify, in writing and individually before any group discussion, the single most consequential decision the organization has been meaning to make and has not made in the past ninety days. The answers are shared without attribution and discussed in the management meeting. This exercise does three things simultaneously: it makes the deferred decision visible as an organizational fact rather than a private concern; it gives every individual in the room permission to name what they have been observing without the social cost of being the one who raises it; and it converts the deferral from a passive organizational condition into a named management problem that can be assigned, resourced, and resolved.

Practice 2, The Named Decision Owner And the Non-Negotiable Deadline

Every consequential decision that has been identified in the deferred decision inventory, or that emerges as requiring resolution in the management process, must have a single named owner and a specific, non negotiable decision deadline. Not a target date. A deadline by which a specific decision, not a recommendation, not a further analysis, a decision, will be made and communicated. The distinction matters because organizations have extensive experience converting decision deadlines into analysis deadlines: the date by which the recommendation will be ready rather than the date by which the decision will be made. The named owner and the non negotiable decision deadline convert the deferred decision into a managed commitment whose non delivery is a performance failure, not a scheduling adjustment.

Practice 3, The Opportunity Cost Calculation

For each significant deferred decision, calculate and explicitly present the specific opportunity cost of continued deferral. Not the cost of making the wrong decision, the cost of making no decision. For a performance decision that has been deferred for six months, estimate the specific strategic work that the underperforming function has not completed, the specific team adaptation that has occurred around the performance gap, and the specific talent at risk because the standard has been demonstrated to be negotiable. For a strategic rationalization decision that has been deferred for a year, estimate the specific capital that has been deployed in the direction being considered for exit rather than in the direction with higher expected return. Making the opportunity cost of deferral visible and specific converts the no decision option from a safe default into a calculable choice whose cost can be compared to the cost of acting.

Practice 4, The Pre Mortem on Continued Avoidance

Apply the pre mortem methodology, described in Chapter Seven of this collection, specifically to the option of continued deferral rather than to the decision being considered. Ask the management team to assume that it is twelve months from today and the organization is significantly worse off because the deferred decision was never made. Have them describe specifically what happened. This exercise produces a different and more actionable picture of the avoidance cost than the opportunity cost calculation, because it names specific competitive and organizational consequences rather than financial abstractions. The pre mortem on continued avoidance makes the cost of the non decision as vivid and as specific as the cost of making the wrong decision, which is the asymmetry that decision avoidance depends on to sustain itself.

Practice 5, The Ceo's Personal Modeling of the Difficult Decision

The most powerful single intervention available to a CEO who wants to create an organization that decides is to make the most difficult deferred decision herself, publicly, with explicit acknowledgment of why it was being avoided and why avoiding it was no longer acceptable. This is not a symbolic gesture. It is a behavioral signal that changes the organizational calculus of deferred decisions for every person who observes it. When the CEO makes the decision that the organization has been collectively avoiding, when he names the performance problem that has been reframed as a development challenge, restructures the customer relationship that has been maintained out of personal history, or exits the strategic direction that has been defended past its evidence based justification, he demonstrates that the social and political cost of making the decision is survivable and that the organizational expectation going forward is that consequential decisions will be made. This demonstration is the only form of cultural change around decision avoidance that I have observed to be durable.

What an Organizationally Decisive Culture Actually Produces

I want to describe what I have observed in the organizations where these practices have been implemented consistently, because the benefits extend well beyond the specific decisions that are made.

The most immediate effect is velocity. An organization that makes consequential decisions at the moment they are ready to be made rather than deferring them until the cost of deferral becomes undeniable operates at a pace that an avoidant organization cannot match. The strategic initiative that was waiting for a personnel decision gets the resources and the leadership it needs weeks rather than months after the need is identified. The capital that was being consumed by an underperforming business unit is redeployed to the high potential initiative without the delay of a twelve month rationalization process. The customer relationships that deserve focused investment receive it rather than sharing management bandwidth with the relationships whose economics do not justify the cost.

The less visible but ultimately more significant effect is on the organization's relationship with its own quality standards. Organizations that consistently defer the difficult decision send a specific signal to every member of the management team: the stated standard and the enforced standard are different. The strategic plan says the company will focus on its highest opportunity activities, but the portfolio rationalization decision keeps being deferred. The performance management framework says underperformance will be addressed within a defined period, but the senior executive has been in the performance improvement plan for two years. The gap between stated and enforced standards produces a specific organizational pathology: the management team stops believing that the organization means what it says, which means they stop holding themselves and their teams to the standards the organization states.

The organization that consistently makes the difficult decisions does not just make better individual decisions. It develops a relationship with its own standards that produces higher performance at every level. People know that the stated expectations are the real expectations. They know that the performance bar is the actual bar. They know that the strategic priority is the genuine priority and not one of seven competing commitments that are all nominally equal. That clarity, produced not by better communication but by consistent follow through on difficult decisions, is the organizational condition in which genuine high performance becomes possible.

I have run companies where the deferred decision culture was the norm and companies where the decisive decision culture was established and maintained. The difference in organizational energy, management team confidence, and ultimately in performance outcomes was not marginal. It was the difference between an organization that is managing its constraints and one that is pursuing its potential. The former is common. The latter is available to any organization whose leadership is willing to make the decisions that determine the difference between the two.

Deciding on time doesn't just improve decisions. It changes what kind of organization you are.

Summary

Decision avoidance in a mid-sized company is not usually a failure of analysis. The issue is known. The information is available. The real barrier is social and political. The avoidance patterns described in this chapter all point to the same fact: the hardest decision is generally the one everyone can identify and no one wants to own. It may involve an executive whose performance no longer fits the role, a business line that should be exited, a customer relationship preserved out of history, or a strategic direction that no longer deserves more capital.

The cost of delay is rarely visible in one reporting period. It accumulates in the opportunities not pursued, the standards not enforced, and the capital not reallocated. Those choices are ultimately expressed most clearly in how the organization pays people. The next chapter turns to incentive structures and shows how compensation built for yesterday can quietly prevent the company from building toward tomorrow.

15

Your Incentive Structure Is Producing Exactly the Results You Don't Want

Compensation is your most powerful tool but most CEOs use it like a landmine instead.

Let me tell you about the most politically sensitive conversation I have had to initiate as a CEO, and I have had to initiate it in some form at every company I have led.

The scenario is always some variation of the same situation. The company has updated its strategic direction, shifted from broad market coverage to vertical focus, from revenue growth to margin expansion, from new customer acquisition to existing customer retention. The strategy is sound. The management team is aligned. The communication has been done well. The planning process produced a clear direction and the board approved it with confidence.

Three quarters later, the behaviors that the strategy requires have not changed at any meaningful level. The salesforce is still chasing the same customer profiles it always chased. The operations team is still optimizing for the same metrics it always optimized for. The marketing function is still generating the same leads it was generating before the strategy changed. The strategy exists in the planning document. It does not exist in the daily decisions of the two hundred people who determine whether it succeeds or fails.

When I ask why, when I sit with the affected managers and have the honest conversation about what is actually driving their decisions, the answer is almost always the same. They are doing what the compensation plan rewards them for doing. Not what the strategy says. Not what the all hands meeting communicated. Not what the strategy poster in the break room declares. What the compensation plan rewards.

This is not disloyalty. It is not strategic resistance. It is rational behavior. People in organizations do what they are paid to do. When the incentive structure and the strategy point in different directions, the incentive structure wins. Every time. Without exception. Because money is the most powerful behavioral direction mechanism available to a CEO, and when it is pointed at the wrong behaviors, no amount of communication, training, or cultural messaging will produce the right ones at scale.

The conversation I then have to initiate, the one about redesigning the compensation structure to align with the current strategy rather than the prior one, is the most politically charged management conversation available in a mid-sized company. It touches on personal income, personal fairness, personal history, and the accumulated expectations of people who have been doing well under the existing arrangement and who will naturally resist any change to it. It is also, in my experience, the single highest leverage management action available to a CEO who is serious about strategy execution.

Compensation is designed for yesterday's strategy. Change the strategy without changing the incentives, and yesterday's behaviors persist.

The Political Reality That Makes This the Hardest Conversation

I want to address the political dimension of compensation management directly, because most management advice on incentive design treats it as a technical problem and underestimates the organizational and human complexity that makes even a well designed compensation change difficult to execute in a mid-sized company.

In a large corporation, compensation changes are managed through a human resources function with institutional processes, compensation benchmarking data, and a defined governance framework that provides cover for the decisions being made. The individual manager may not like the outcome, but the process has a legitimacy that makes the decision feel less personal.

In a mid-sized company, compensation is intensely personal in ways that large company management often forgets. The senior salesperson has known the CEO since the company had twelve employees. His compensation arrangement was negotiated directly with the founder, at a moment when the company needed him and was willing to make commitments to retain him. The operating manager's compensation reflects a verbal agreement made three years ago that was never put in writing but that both parties remember clearly. The finance director's bonus formula has been the same for four years because changing it would require a conversation that nobody has been willing to have.

These are not exceptional arrangements. They are the normal accumulation of compensation decisions in a company that has grown organically, made hiring decisions under time pressure, and managed relationships with the intimacy of a small organization. Every person in the senior team has a compensation story, and every compensation story has a political context. Changing any element of the structure touches every story simultaneously, even if the change only directly affects a subset of them.

I am not describing this complexity as a reason not to address the misalignment. I am describing it as the reason most CEOs defer the address for longer than the misalignment cost justifies, and as the context that the specific practices I recommend at the end of this article are designed for.

Compensation is the most charged conversation in the building — and the most important one for a CEO who wants the strategy to be more than a document.

How the Misalignment Forms: The Natural Drift Between Compensation and Strategy

Incentive misalignment does not arrive as a design error. It arrives as a natural consequence of organizational growth and strategic evolution in companies that address compensation reactively rather than strategically.

The compensation structure of a mid-sized company at forty million dollars in revenue is almost never the result of a compensation design. It is the result of a compensation history: the plan that was put in place when the company needed to attract a specific hire, modified slightly when that hire negotiated a retention arrangement, supplemented with a bonus structure that made sense at the time and has been renewed annually without reassessment, adjusted at the margins for market conditions without ever being evaluated against strategic alignment.

The result is a compensation architecture that is optimized for the behaviors that mattered most at each historical moment when a compensation decision was made, and that has not been evaluated against the behaviors that the current strategy requires. The sales compensation plan rewards the behavior that was most important when revenue growth was the primary strategic objective. The operations compensation plan rewards the efficiency metrics that mattered when cost reduction was the primary management priority. The management team bonus plan rewards the milestones that the board was focused on two years ago.

None of these plans are wrong in the abstract. All of them are misaligned with the current strategy in the specific. And the specific misalignment, embedded in every paycheck and every quarterly bonus calculation, is more powerful than any strategy communication program the company can run.

The Five Incentive Misalignments That Most Damage mid-sized Company Strategy Execution

In my experience leading and advising mid-sized companies across multiple sectors, five specific incentive misalignments appear with enough regularity to be considered structural rather than situational. Each one is the product of a rational compensation decision made at an earlier stage of the company's development that has outlasted its alignment with the company's current strategic direction.

Misalignment 1, Revenue Based Sales Compensation When Margin Is the Strategic Priority

How it forms: The sales compensation plan was designed when revenue growth was the primary strategic objective. The commission structure pays a flat percentage of revenue on every sale regardless of margin. The strategic priority has shifted to margin expansion, a result of compressed gross margins, a strategic decision to focus on higher value customer segments, or a recognition that revenue growth at current margins is destroying rather than creating enterprise value. The commission plan has not changed.

The behavior it produces: The salesforce continues optimizing for revenue. They discount aggressively to win the deal because the commission is on revenue, not margin. They pursue the large volume, low margin account because the commission dollar is the same regardless of the margin contribution. They avoid the small volume, high margin opportunity because the commission is lower even though the margin contribution is higher. Every individual salesperson is doing exactly what the compensation plan asks them to do. Every individual salesperson is acting against the strategy.

The strategic cost: The gap between the salesforce behavior the strategy requires and the behavior the compensation plan produces is not a sales management problem. It is a compensation design problem. Adding more sales management, more training, or more strategy communication will not change the behavior because it does not change the incentive. The behavior will change only when the commission structure changes. On a thirty million dollar revenue business, the difference between the current margin performance and the margin performance the strategy requires is frequently two to four margin points, representing six hundred thousand to one point two million dollars of annual EBITDA that the compensation misalignment is actively preventing.

Misalignment 2, New Customer Acquisition Incentives When Retention Is the Strategic Priority

How it forms: The company has reached a scale at which net revenue retention, the expansion and retention of the existing customer base, is more valuable per dollar of investment than new customer acquisition. Customer acquisition costs have risen as the most accessible market segments have been addressed. The existing customer base has expansion potential that is significantly underinvested. The strategic priority is to grow from within the current customer portfolio. The incentive structure continues paying significantly higher rates for new customer acquisition than for existing customer expansion.

The behavior it produces: The salesforce directs its time and energy toward new customer acquisition because the incentive structure makes it more financially rewarding. The account management team, compensated on a flat salary or a modest retention bonus, has no financial motivation to pursue the expansion conversations that the strategy identifies as the primary growth driver. The customers who have been with the company for three years and who have significant expansion potential receive less creative sales attention than the prospect who has never purchased from the company.

The strategic cost: Customer expansion is systematically more efficient than customer acquisition in most mid-sized service and technology businesses at this stage of development. Existing customers have lower acquisition cost, higher conversion rates, faster sales cycles, and higher lifetime value than equivalent new customers. The company whose compensation structure does not reflect this efficiency is investing its most expensive organizational resource, senior salesperson time, in the highest cost growth activity rather than the highest return one.

Misalignment 3, Volume Based Operations Incentives When Quality and Customer Experience Are the Strategic Priority

How it forms: The operations team is compensated on throughput: units processed, cases handled, tickets closed, orders fulfilled. The metrics reflect the priority that existed when operational capacity was the binding constraint. The strategic priority has shifted to service quality and customer experience, the recognition that customer retention is determined by the quality of the delivery experience rather than the speed of the delivery itself. The throughput metrics remain.

The behavior it produces: The operations team optimizes for volume because that is what their compensation rewards. Customer complaints that require time to resolve properly are closed quickly to maintain the ticket closure rate. Exceptions that require individual attention are handled by the most efficient process rather than the most appropriate one. The customer whose problem requires a non standard approach receives the standard approach because the standard approach is what the throughput metric measures. The operations team is performing exactly as they are compensated to perform. The customer experience reflects the incentive, not the strategy.

The strategic cost: The long term cost of customer experience delivered by a volume optimizing operations team is customer attrition that does not appear in the management reporting immediately but that compounds through the customer lifetime value erosion that reduced retention produces. In a company where each customer represents several years of recurring revenue, a one percentage point reduction in annual retention rate represents a meaningful reduction in the net present value of the customer base. The operations incentive that produces the retention reduction is costing the company more in customer lifetime value than it is saving in operational efficiency.

Misalignment 4, Individual Contribution Incentives When Cross Functional Collaboration Is the Strategic Priority

How it forms: The bonus structure rewards individual performance against individual targets. The strategy requires cross functional collaboration to execute: product development needs customer success input to build the right features; sales needs operations input to make commitments the company can deliver; marketing needs finance input to allocate the budget where it will produce the highest return. The individual contribution bonus creates competitive rather than collaborative dynamics between the functions that the strategy requires to work together.

The behavior it produces: Each function optimizes for its own metrics at the expense of the collaborative outcomes the strategy requires. Sales makes customer commitments that operations cannot deliver because the sales bonus is on the deal and the consequences of the delivery failure are borne by operations. Product makes roadmap decisions without customer success input because the product bonus is on features shipped rather than on customer adoption. Finance imposes budget restrictions on marketing without understanding the revenue implications because the finance bonus is on cost control rather than revenue optimization. Each function is performing against its own incentive plan. The company is performing below what cross functional alignment would produce.

The strategic cost: The collaboration tax, the performance foregone because functions are optimizing against each other rather than together, is among the most consistently underestimated costs in mid-sized company management. In companies where strategy execution requires sustained cross functional alignment, the absence of collaborative incentives can reduce the pace of strategic execution by thirty to fifty percent relative to what a well aligned incentive structure would produce.

Misalignment 5, Short Term Performance Incentives When Long Term Value Creation Is the Strategic Priority

How it forms: The bonus plan is annual. Payouts are based on this year's performance against this year's targets. The company is at a stage of development where the most important investments, in management depth, in customer relationship quality, in technology infrastructure, in brand positioning, have payback periods of two to four years. The decisions that will determine the company's value in five years are being made by managers whose compensation is entirely determined by this year's results.

The behavior it produces: Managers make decisions that optimize for the current year's performance metrics at the expense of the investments that would produce superior multi year outcomes. Training and development budgets are cut when the quarterly revenue target is at risk because the training cost is immediate and the capability improvement is delayed. Customer relationship investments that would improve three year retention but reduce this year's cost ratio are deprioritized. Capital investments with 24 month payback periods are delayed in favor of short term cost reduction that improves the current year EBITDA bonus calculation.

The strategic cost: The cumulative effect of short term incentive driven decision making in a mid-sized company is a systematic underinvestment in the capabilities, relationships, and infrastructure that determine the company's medium term competitive position. This underinvestment is invisible in the current year's financial statements, which show improved margins from the cost reductions. It is visible in the three year competitive position, the customer retention trend, and the enterprise value that a sophisticated buyer will calculate based on the quality and trajectory of the business rather than its current year metrics.

The Incentive Alignment Audit: Finding Your Own Misalignment

Before recommending any compensation redesign, I recommend that every CEO of a mid-sized company conduct an incentive alignment audit, a structured examination of the gap between what the current compensation structure rewards and what the current strategy requires. This audit is not a compensation benchmarking exercise. It is a behavioral analysis: given the incentives currently in place, what specific behaviors are being produced, and are those behaviors what the strategy needs?

The audit has four steps.

Audit Step	Specific Questions and Method
Step 1: List the behaviors the strategy requires	For each major function, sales, operations, product, finance, customer success, list the three to five specific behaviors that, if performed consistently by everyone in that function, would produce the strategic outcomes the company is seeking. Be specific: not 'focus on high value customers 'but spend sixty percent of prospecting time on accounts with more than fifty employees in the target verticals.' Not 'improve customer experience' but 'resolve every customer complaint requiring a policy exception within twenty four hours by escalating directly to the account manager rather than routing through the standard ticket queue.'
Step 2: Map the current incentive against each required behavior	For each behavior identified in Step 1, examine the current compensation structure and answer: does the current incentive make this behavior more likely, less likely, or neutral? A compensation plan that makes a required behavior less likely is a misalignment. A plan that is neutral to a required behavior is an opportunity. The result of this mapping is the specific list of misalignments that the compensation redesign must address.
Step 3: Identify the behaviors the current incentive produces but the strategy does not require	This is the reverse mapping: given the current incentive structure, what behaviors are being rewarded that the strategy does not require? These are the legacy behaviors, the ones that mattered under the prior strategy and that continue to be incentivized by an unreformed compensation plan. The elimination of these incentives is as important as the addition of new aligned ones, because legacy incentives create organizational confusion when they coexist with new strategic direction.
Step 4: Calculate the cost of the misalignment	For each significant misalignment identified, estimate the specific financial or strategic cost. The margin gap produced by the revenue based sales commission. The customer lifetime value reduction produced by the retention deficit in the acquisition focused incentive structure. The collaborative tax produced by the individual contribution bonus in a cross functional strategy. These estimates do not need to be precise. They need to be credible enough to justify the political cost of the compensation redesign.

The audit typically takes a half day to complete rigorously. What it produces is not a compensation design, it is the business case for a compensation redesign. And having the business case before entering the political conversation about compensation change is the most important preparation available to the CEO who is about to have the most charged conversation in the building.

Managing the Politics: The Conversation That Cannot Be Avoided

I want to be direct about the political reality of compensation redesign in a mid-sized company, because the executive who approaches it naively, with the assumption that a well designed compensation plan will be received on its merits, will be surprised by the resistance and will likely retreat to a compromise that preserves the misalignment while creating the organizational impression that the issue has been addressed.

The compensation redesign will be experienced by some members of the team as a reduction in their earning potential. Even if the redesign is carefully structured so that high performers who align with the new strategic direction earn at least as much as they did under the old structure, the people whose behavior must change most significantly to capture the new incentives will experience the redesign as a threat to their current income. Their reaction will be rational and predictable: they will argue that the new metrics are unfair, that the targets are unrealistic, that the transition period is too short, and that the change signals a lack of appreciation for their past contributions.

These arguments will be made to the CEO directly, in sidebar conversations with peers, and in the informal influence networks that exist in every mid-sized company and that have more influence on organizational culture than any formal management process. Ignoring them does not make them less effective. Managing them requires a specific approach that I have developed through direct experience with the political dynamics of compensation change.

Principle 1: Transparency About the Why Before the What

The CEO who announces a compensation change before explaining the strategic logic that requires it will face maximum political resistance. Every person affected will fill the explanation vacuum with their own interpretation, and the interpretations will not be favorable. Present the misalignment analysis, specifically, the gap between what the current incentive structure produces and what the strategy requires, to the full management team before presenting any proposed changes. Make the business case visible. Let the team see the same picture you are seeing. This does not eliminate resistance, but it changes the nature of the resistance from 'the CEO is changing our pay' to 'our current incentives are producing behaviors that are working against the strategy we all agreed on.' That is a more manageable conversation.

Principle 2: Transition Periods That Are Genuinely Transitional

The most common structural error in compensation redesigns is the abrupt cutover: on a specific date, the old plan ends and the new plan begins. For people who have been performing well under the old plan, the abrupt cutover feels punitive even when the new plan is objectively fair. Structure transition periods that allow people to adapt their behaviors before their income is fully exposed to the new metrics. A partial transition, in which the compensation for the first year reflects both the old and the new incentive structure in defined proportions, reduces the income risk during the adaptation period and gives people a genuine opportunity to demonstrate alignment with the new direction before the full financial consequences of the transition are felt.

Principle 3: Individual Conversations Before Group Announcements

Compensation change should be communicated first in individual conversations between the CEO or the direct manager and each affected person, before any group announcement. The group announcement should describe what is changing and why. The individual conversation should address the specific implications for that person's total compensation, the specific behaviors that will generate the highest income under the new structure, and the specific support the company will provide to help the person make the transition. This sequence respects the personal nature of compensation, reduces the emotional heat of the group announcement by giving people time to process the implications privately, and allows the CEO to address the specific concerns of the people whose cooperation is most critical to the transition's success.

Principle 4: The High Performer Who Will Not Adapt

Every compensation redesign will surface at least one high performer under the old structure who is unwilling or unable to adapt to the new one. This person is the most politically difficult element of the transition because their historical performance record makes it easy to argue that the new incentive structure is wrong rather than that their behavioral adaptation is required. The CEO who makes an exception for this person, who provides a protected compensation arrangement that insulates them from the new strategic incentives, has effectively signaled to the entire organization that the new incentive structure is negotiable for people with sufficient organizational leverage. The exception undermines the entire redesign. Managing the high performer who will not adapt requires the same decision making clarity described in the article on decision avoidance: the performance record from the prior strategy does not override the behavioral requirement of the current one.

Five Practices That Produce Incentive Alignment in mid-sized Companies

The following practices address both the design challenge and the implementation challenge of incentive realignment. They are presented in the order in which they should be applied.

Practice 1, Run the Incentive Alignment Audit Annually, Not Reactively

The compensation misalignment described in this article forms gradually, through the natural drift between a compensation plan designed at one point in time and a strategy that has evolved since that design. The company that catches this drift annually, before it has produced significant behavioral misalignment, makes compensation adjustments that are smaller, less disruptive, and less politically charged than the company that addresses the drift only when the misalignment has become acute. Make the incentive alignment audit a standing annual management discipline, conducted at the same time as the strategic planning process, with the explicit objective of identifying gaps between the current incentive structure and the current strategic direction before those gaps produce organizational consequences.

Practice 2, Design Every Incentive Plan with A Behavioral Description, Not Just A Metric

The most common error in mid-sized company incentive design is the metric without a behavioral description. The commission is set as a percentage of revenue. The bonus is set as a percentage of EBITDA. The metric is clear. The behavior it produces is not examined. Every incentive plan should be accompanied by a written behavioral description: given this incentive structure, what specific decisions will the people in this role make differently than they would without the incentive? If the behavioral description does not match the behaviors the strategy requires, the metric is wrong. Designing backward from the required behavior to the metric that produces it is more difficult than setting a convenient financial target, and it produces compensation plans that are far more strategically effective.

Practice 3, Add A Collaborative Component to Every Individual Incentive Plan

Every compensation plan in a mid-sized company should contain both an individual performance component and a shared company or team performance component. The shared component need not be large, fifteen to twenty five percent of variable compensation is sufficient to change the organizational dynamic from competitive to collaborative. When part of every person's income depends on outcomes that require other functions to perform well, the compensation structure creates a financial stake in cross functional success that no amount of cultural messaging or management instruction can replicate. The specific shared metric should be chosen at the company level, EBITDA margin, net revenue retention, customer satisfaction score, based on the outcome that most directly reflects the strategy's success.

Practice 4, Include At Least One Multi Year Metric in Every Senior Leader's Compensation

For every member of the senior management team, the compensation plan should include at least one metric that has a two to three year measurement period. This metric should reflect the most important investment the company is making in its medium term competitive position: management team capability, customer base quality, technology infrastructure, or brand position. The specific metric matters less than the principle: when part of a senior leader's income is measured over multiple years, they make the investments in medium term value creation that a purely annual incentive structure systematically underproduces. This does not require complex deferred compensation or equity structures. It requires setting a specific metric, measuring it annually, and paying the associated incentive when the multi year target is achieved.

Practice 5, Review the Compensation Plan in Every Strategic Planning Session

The strategic planning session is the moment when the management team articulates where the company is going and what it must do differently to get there. It is also the moment when the management team is most clearly aware of the specific behaviors the strategy requires. Make the incentive alignment audit a mandatory output of the strategic planning session: before the planning session concludes, the management team should explicitly confirm that the existing compensation structure rewards the behaviors identified as strategic requirements, and should identify any gaps that the plan in the following year must address. This practice prevents the compensation drift that produces the misalignment, not by designing a perfect compensation plan, but by ensuring that the compensation plan and the strategy are reviewed together frequently enough that the drift cannot accumulate to consequence.

What Incentive Alignment Actually Produces

I want to close with something concrete, because the incentive alignment conversation can seem abstract when it is described in terms of design principles and audit protocols. The practical experience of a management team that has made the transition from misaligned to aligned compensation is specific and immediate in ways that the design language does not capture.

The most immediate change is conversational. When the compensation structure is aligned with the strategy, the management conversation changes character. Managers stop arguing at the margin of the old strategy and start asking questions about how to execute the new one most effectively. The sales manager who was resistant to the vertical focus strategy becomes genuinely interested in which verticals offer the highest commission opportunity under the new plan. The operations manager who was defending the throughput metrics starts asking what the new quality metrics are and how they will be measured. The compensation alignment does not produce strategic enthusiasm through inspiration. It produces it through financial interest. And financial interest is significantly more durable than inspiration as a driver of sustained behavioral change.

The second change is strategic credibility. In my experience, the single most important signal that a mid-sized company's leadership can send about the seriousness of a new strategic direction is putting compensation behind it. A strategy that is communicated through presentations, posters, and all hands meetings but that is not reflected in the compensation structure sends a specific organizational message:

this is what management believes is strategically important, but not important enough to affect anyone's paycheck. That message is received and decoded accurately by every member of the management team within the first quarter.

Conversely, a strategy that is reflected in the compensation structure sends an equally specific message: management believes this direction is important enough to put money on it. The incentive alignment converts the strategic direction from a management aspiration into an organizational commitment. It is the difference between a strategy that is stated and a strategy that is real.

The third change is retention of the right people. Compensation realignment is, among other things, a sorting mechanism. The people whose capabilities and motivations are well suited to the new strategic direction will thrive under an incentive structure that rewards the behaviors that direction requires. The people whose capabilities and motivations are better suited to the prior direction will struggle and, over time, will self select toward organizations whose compensation structure matches their natural work orientation. This sorting is not always comfortable in the short term, some high performers under the old structure will be the people who leave, but it is the mechanism through which the organization builds the talent base that the new strategy requires.

I have initiated the compensation realignment conversation in every company I have led, and I have never found it easy. The political complexity is real, the relational cost is real, and the short term disruption is real. What is also real is the difference in the organization's strategic execution before and after the alignment. The company whose compensation structure and strategic direction point the same way is a company that can execute at a pace and a quality that the misaligned company cannot match, because it is a company where every paycheck is an argument for the strategy.

Aligning compensation doesn't take more money. It takes the courage to point the money where the strategy demands — and only the CEO can do that.

Summary

The incentive misalignment in this chapter resembles the capital structure mismatch described earlier in the book. Both are the residue of reasonable past decisions that continue shaping present behavior long after their original logic has expired. Both often remain invisible while producing highly visible consequences. And both can be corrected only through deliberate redesign, not through gradual drift.

The core truth is simple. Money points somewhere, and the organization follows. If compensation still rewards the old strategy, the company will continue producing old strategy behavior regardless of what leadership now says it wants. Redesigning incentives is politically difficult because it touches history, identity, and income all at once. But a CEO who does not do it is leaving the most powerful behavior shaping tool in the company aimed in the wrong direction.

The next chapter asks whether the board overseeing all of this, the avoided decisions, the misaligned incentives, and the gap between presentation and reality, actually sees what is happening in the business it governs.

16

What the Board Sees and What Is Actually Happening Are Usually Different Things

The gap isn't a lie; it's built into governance itself, and closing it takes work from both sides.

I have sat in a great many board meetings. As chairman of two public companies, as an independent director on several others, and earlier in my career as the CEO on the presenting side of the table, I have seen the same governance event from every angle it can be observed.

That experience taught me a discipline I was not taught and did not develop quickly: listen with equal intensity to what is said, what is not said, what is said more carefully than the subject warrants, and what is delivered with a smoothness that suggests the rough edges were worked out before the meeting began.

Most board members listen mainly to the first category. That is understandable. The materials are dense, the meeting is short, and the formal obligation is to the information that has been transmitted. But the most important information is often not in the presentation itself. It lives in the gap between the presentation and the reality.

It shows up in the metric that was in last quarter's package and is absent from this quarter's without explanation. It appears in the answer that is longer and more careful than the question required. It appears in the topic that is introduced with unusual formality when it was historically discussed with ease. It appears in the competitive development described in the passive voice when every other development was described in the active one.

This chapter is about that gap, the distance between what the board sees and what is actually happening, and about the specific disciplines that allow both sides of the governance relationship to close it. I write it from both perspectives: from the chairman's chair, where I learned to read the signals the presentation did not intend to send, and from the executive's chair, where I learned how the dynamics of board reporting shape what arrives and how that dynamic can be managed constructively.

The board deck isn't a window. It's a curation — and boards that forget the difference see a better company than the one they govern.

Why the Gap Exists

The gap between the board presentation and the operational reality is not primarily a product of dishonesty. I have rarely sat in a board meeting with management that was deliberately misleading the board. What I have seen regularly is management presenting the business through a lens shaped by the structure of the governance relationship, in ways that systematically distort the board's picture without anyone intending to distort it.

The first dynamic is the approval seeking orientation built into the relationship. Management presents to the board. The board approves or challenges. Management knows, at some level, that approval is easier than challenge. That knowledge affects the presentation. Information likely to generate confidence gets more emphasis and more completeness than information likely to generate friction. The strongest quarter gets several slides. The weakest strategic development gets a brief paragraph and a recovery plan.

The second dynamic is expertise asymmetry. Management has been inside the business every day for the past quarter. The board has been inside it for several hours. Management knows what happened. The board learns what management chose to present about what happened. This asymmetry is not avoidable in the short term, but it means the board's picture is always a curated subset of management's picture.

The third dynamic is the social contract of the senior team. When the CFO presents the quarter, the Chief Revenue Officer usually does not interrupt to say the revenue was flattered by a pricing action that will not hold. When the CEO presents the strategy, the Chief Operating Officer usually does not note that the capacity required to execute it does not yet exist. The board receives a unified management view of the business. The disagreements, doubts, and minority views are typically resolved before the board sees them.

Management presents what the team agreed to say, not what its members actually think. The board's job is to know the difference.

What I Have Learned to Listen For

The missing metric

Every reporting package contains a set of metrics the company has chosen to track. When a metric that appeared last quarter disappears this quarter, I notice before any other question is asked. The absence of a metric is often more informative than its presence. Metrics disappear when they begin telling a story management would prefer not to tell in a board forum.

My practice when I notice a missing metric is not to demand it immediately in the room. That often produces defensiveness. I note it, ask for it in writing before the next session, and pay close attention to what the response reveals about why the metric disappeared.

The passive voice construction

Management teams communicate urgency and ownership through grammar. A problem described in the active voice, for example, "we lost a significant customer account in Q3 because our service delivery did not meet the contractual requirement," is a problem management has owned. A problem described in the passive voice, for example, "a customer account was concluded in Q3 following a service performance issue," is a problem management is still managing around.

When I hear that construction, I usually engage it directly: "You said the account was concluded. Can you walk me through what happened from the company's side?" The move from passive to active often forces the discussion into the substance that the original answer avoided.

The overly careful answer

Most board questions receive answers that are broadly proportional to the complexity of the question. When a simple question generates an answer that is unusually long, heavily qualified, and carefully hedged, I assume the subject touches something management has thought carefully about how to discuss.

The care itself is the signal. It usually means there is something in that subject area that management is managing tightly in the board setting. My follow up is not to challenge the answer directly. It is to ask a different question about the same subject and observe what the unrehearsed response reveals.

The forward focused reframe

One of the most common patterns in board materials is the move from current problem to future solution before the current problem has been fully examined. The revenue shortfall is presented alongside the recovery plan before the board has understood why the shortfall occurred. The operational failure is presented with the remediation initiative before the board has grasped the full scope of the problem.

My practice is to interrupt that pivot politely but clearly. "Before we discuss the recovery plan, I would like to understand what happened in Q3 specifically. Can you walk us through the causes of the shortfall?" The past contains the information required to evaluate the future. A board that moves forward too quickly is accepting a frame that may not serve its oversight role.

The Five Information Gaps That Most Affect mid-sized Company Boards

1. Forward revenue signal versus trailing revenue report

What the board usually sees is a backward looking revenue picture: year to date totals, quarter over quarter comparisons, and performance against plan. Those numbers are useful and usually accurate.

What often remains underrepresented is the forward revenue signal: pipeline quality, pipeline velocity, conversion rates, and the condition of the opportunities that will determine next quarter's results. By the time a weak pipeline produces a revenue shortfall in the reported results, the window for intervention has often closed.

The chairman's question is straightforward: "How does the current pipeline compare with the pipeline we had at this point last year before the equivalent quarter?" If the answer is vague, or if the data is not readily available, the pipeline discipline may be weaker than the current revenue trend suggests.

2. Customer health signal versus revenue retention report

Boards are often shown customer retention as a rate. The metric is useful, but it is also blunt. What it does not typically show is which specific accounts are quietly weakening, which service patterns are deteriorating, and which relationships are becoming vulnerable before the numbers reflect it.

The more useful board questions are account specific. "What is the retention rate for the top twenty accounts?" and "Which of those accounts have shown reduced purchase frequency or reduced volume in the past two quarters?" A healthy blended retention figure can conceal a looming problem in the company's largest relationships.

3. Management team reality versus organizational chart

The board is usually shown the organizational chart and given a broad description of the leadership team. What it rarely receives, unless it asks directly, is a candid assessment of performance distribution within the team: which functions are independently strong, which are adequate, and which are being stabilized by the CEO's continued involvement.

A board should ask at least once a year for a management depth assessment that addresses performance, independent capability, and succession status for each critical role. A CEO who can answer that question candidly is usually a CEO the board can trust more broadly.

4. Strategic execution reality versus initiative status report

Many boards receive detailed initiative reports: milestones, timelines, budgets, and work completed. Those reports describe whether management is executing a plan. They do not necessarily show whether the company is moving closer to the competitive position the strategy was supposed to create.

Once each year, the board should require a more strategic question: "Given everything executed in the last twelve months, are we materially closer to the competitive position this strategy was designed to achieve?" That question separates tactical progress from strategic outcome.

5. Financial quality signal versus financial performance report

Revenue, gross margin, EBITDA, and cash flow can all be accurately reported while still failing to explain the quality of the quarter. How much of the result is recurring? How much of the margin improvement is structural? How much of the cash flow strength came from timing rather than operating performance?

The chairman's most useful version of this question is often directed to the CFO rather than the CEO: "Of the EBITDA reported this quarter, how much do you consider fully recurring at the current run rate, and how much reflects one time or timing related items?" The difference between performance and performance quality is where many governance blind spots begin.

What Executives Owe the Board

I spent enough years on the executive side of the table to understand that the instinct to present the business in its best light is not a moral weakness. It is the natural response of a person who cares about the company, feels responsible for its outcomes, and is aware that every board meeting contains an implicit evaluation.

But the executives who build the strongest governance relationships are not the ones who always present good news. They are the ones who present a complete picture, including the uncomfortable parts, consistently enough that the board comes to trust the reporting rather than interrogate it.

That trust has real value. A board that trusts the completeness of management's reporting makes decisions faster and with less friction. It spends less time probing for what it suspects is missing and more time helping management think strategically. A board that does not trust the completeness of the reporting consumes time, energy, and political capital in ways that make governance worse for everyone involved.

The board that trusts management's reporting is not the board that receives only good news. It is the board that receives complete news, including the uncomfortable parts, often enough to believe that what it sees is what is actually there.

Six Practices That Close the Governance Information Gap

1. The pre meeting chairman's question

Before every board meeting, the chairman should send one specific question about something noticed in the materials. The purpose is not to challenge management in advance. It is to create an opening for a more thoughtful and more complete answer than the board book alone contains.

2. The independent operating view

At least twice a year, outside the formal meeting cadence, the chairman should speak directly with senior operators who do not usually present to the board. Those conversations should be transparent and known to the CEO. Their value is the operational texture they reveal, not any circumvention of management authority.

3. The metric commitment protocol

At the beginning of each fiscal year, the board and management should agree on the core metrics that will appear in every package for the next twelve months regardless of whether their direction is favorable. This reduces selective omission and makes the reporting more trustworthy over time.

4. The CEO's bad news discipline

Every board presentation should contain at least one piece of genuinely uncomfortable information. That discipline changes the relationship between the board and the presentation. The board stops assuming the hard news must be dug out and begins trusting that it will be surfaced.

5. The competitive environment briefing

At least quarterly, the board should receive an external or at least independently framed view of the competitive environment rather than relying only on the management team executing the current strategy. The point is not to challenge management reflexively. It is to ensure the board has enough independent perspective to govern well.

6. The annual governance audit

Once each year, the board should ask explicitly whether the information it receives is adequate for its responsibilities. Are there issues it does not understand well enough? Are there questions directors have been meaning to ask? Are there topics discussed privately but not raised formally? Governance improves when those uncertainties are made visible before they become failures.

The Adversarial Trap

The most common objection to all of this is that a board with more complete information, more independent views, and more probing discipline will become adversarial. The risk is real, but it is not caused by better information. It is caused by suspicion replacing trust.

The practices above are not designed to produce suspicion. They are designed to produce transparency, which only a trusting relationship can sustain over time. The chairman who asks the pre meeting question is not accusing management of hiding information. He is creating a path for fuller disclosure. The CEO who includes genuinely bad news in the presentation is not inviting punishment. he is demonstrating the courage that earns confidence.

The most functional governance relationships I have known share one trait: the board knows things that make it uncomfortable, management knows the board knows them, and neither side treats that knowledge as a threat. The difficult customer relationship, the weak management depth in one function, the strategic bet that is not developing as planned, all of it is discussable. That is what real governance partnership looks like.

A board's value isn't oversight. It's perspective — and perspective requires information complete enough to trust.

Summary

The governance information gap described here is structural, not personal. It comes from the approval seeking nature of management presentation, the expertise asymmetry built into oversight, and the management team's natural tendency to resolve disagreement before it reaches the board. None of that requires dishonesty. It requires only ordinary human behavior inside the incentives of the governance relationship.

The disciplines outlined in this chapter, from the pre meeting chairman's question to the bad news discipline and the independent operating view, are not designed to create a more adversarial board. They are meant to create the information environment in which the board and management can actually become strategic partners. That matters most in the final stage of the book's arc, when everything the previous chapters have addressed either shows up as strength or is exposed as unfinished work.

The next chapter examines the two years before an exit, the period when the whole accumulated story of the company is repriced through the lens of recency, preparation, and trajectory.

17

Private Equity Finds What You Have Not Fixed And Prices It Accordingly

DEFERRED PROBLEMS AREN'T HIDDEN FROM BUYERS — THEY'RE PRICED BY THEM.

I have sat on the buying side of the table in enough private equity and sponsor review processes to have formed a clear and consistent view of how the most damaging moments in a liquidity event occur. They are not usually the result of a failing business. They are not usually the result of a dishonest owner. They are almost always the result of an owner who walked into a sophisticated capital process carrying problems he knew existed, believed he could manage around, and discovered that he could not.

The investment banker presentations are often solid. The market analysis is credible. The growth narrative is compelling. The management team can articulate the strategic direction with fluency and confidence. And yet, somewhere in the diligence process, always in the diligence process, the things that were not addressed before the process started become the things that determine the final price, the deal structure, or whether the transaction closes at all.

I have seen this from both directions. As a sponsor and private equity participant reviewing hundreds of companies, I sat on the side that found the problems. As an operating advisor and principal investor who helps founders prepare for capital events, I now sit on the side that helps owners find and fix those problems before a buyer does. The view from both sides has given me a specific and practical understanding of what private equity finds in every deal they look at seriously, and what it costs owners who let the diligence team find it rather than finding it themselves.

This article is for the owner or CEO who is approaching a liquidity event, a private equity recapitalization, a strategic sale, a management buyout, or a growth capital raise, and who wants to understand, in direct terms, what the process will surface and what the commercial consequence of each finding will be. It is not theoretical. It is the account of what I have watched happen, repeatedly and predictably, in transactions involving mid-sized companies in the range most relevant to the HBR audience: fifteen million to two hundred million dollars in enterprise value.

Every deferred problem in your business is a discount. The only question is whether you apply it early, or the buyer applies it late — when your leverage is gone.

How Private Equity Diligence Actually Works, What Most Owners Do Not Know

Most owners who have not previously been through a private equity process have a mental model of diligence that is shaped by the investment banker's description of it: a structured, time limited review of financial, legal, and commercial information that validates the business before the transaction closes. This mental model is accurate as a description of what diligence is supposed to look like. It is significantly incomplete as a description of what it actually is.

What diligence actually is, from the buyer's perspective, is a systematic search for risk. Not the kind of risk that is disclosed in the offering memorandum or the management presentation. The kind of risk that has been accumulated over the life of the business through decisions that seemed individually reasonable and that, in aggregate, represent a picture of the company that is materially different from the one the management presentation describes.

Private equity firms employ three parallel diligence workstreams that operate simultaneously during a transaction process. The financial diligence team, typically a quality of earnings firm engaged by the buyer, reconstructs the financial statements with the specific objective of identifying the gap between reported EBITDA and sustainable EBITDA. The commercial diligence team validates the market opportunity and competitive position through independent research, customer interviews, and competitive mapping that the management team does not participate in designing. And the operational and management diligence team, often conducted by the PE firm's operating partners rather than by outside advisors, assesses the quality, depth, and independence of the management team and the operational systems that support the business's performance.

These three workstreams do not accept management representations at face value. They verify them. The customer reference calls are not the references the management team suggests, they are calls made to customers the diligence team identifies independently. The management team assessment is not a review of the organization chart, it is a direct evaluation of whether each member of the senior team can perform their function independently of the founder. The market analysis is not a review of the industry reports in the data room, it is an independent reconstruction of the competitive dynamics in the specific markets the company operates in.

For an owner who has not been through this process before, the experience can be genuinely disorienting. The transaction, which felt like a negotiation over the value of something he built, becomes a diagnostic process in which every assumption about the business's quality is tested by a team of professionals whose financial incentive is to find what the management presentation understated.

Diligence isn't there to confirm your story. It's there to find the gap between your story and your numbers.

The Five Findings That Appear in Almost Every mid-sized Company Transaction

Having reviewed hundreds of companies as a sponsor and investor, and having advised dozens of owners through the preparation for capital processes, I can describe the specific findings that appear with enough consistency to be considered structural rather than situational. These are not exotic problems. They are the ordinary accumulation of how owner managed businesses are built and run, and they are the findings that private equity prices most directly and most aggressively.

For each finding, I describe what the PE firm's diligence team discovers, what the price impact is on the transaction, and what the owner could have done in the two to three years before the process started to convert the finding from a buyer discount into a seller advantage.

Finding 1, EBITDA Quality and Normalization Gaps

What PE finds in diligence: The quality of earnings firm reconstructs the financial statements and identifies the gap between reported EBITDA and what a buyer can rely on as the true recurring earnings of the business. The gap includes owner compensation above market rate, personal expenses flowing through the business, above market related party arrangements, non recurring items that are actually recurring in character, and revenue recognition timing that inflates any given period's results at the expense of the adjacent one. In a typical mid-sized transaction in the $20M to $80M enterprise value range, this gap is between fifteen and thirty five percent of reported EBITDA.

The price impact: The EBITDA normalization gap has a compounding price impact that most owners do not anticipate. It reduces the base EBITDA on which the multiple is applied, that is the direct impact. But it also signals to the buyer that the financial reporting quality of the business is insufficient to support full confidence in the forward projections. The combination of a lower EBITDA base and a compressed multiple applied to that base typically produces a total price reduction of twenty to forty percent relative to the owner's expectation. On a transaction with an expected enterprise value of $50M, this is a $10M to $20M gap that appears in the final round of negotiation.

The pre process remedy: Commission a quality of earnings analysis, prepared to buyer diligence standards, covering the prior three fiscal years. Not six months before the process starts, three years before. The three years of clean financial track record that results from this exercise, market rate compensation, no personal expenses in the business P&L, no above market related party arrangements, produces a normalized

EBITDA that the buyer cannot reconstruct away from. The finding becomes a verification rather than a revision.

Finding 2, Customer Concentration and Revenue Quality Risks

What PE finds in diligence: The commercial diligence team maps the revenue base with a specificity that the management presentation's customer list does not provide. They calculate the revenue concentration: what percentage of total revenue is generated by the top three, five, and ten customers. They assess the contractual basis of each major relationship: is the revenue protected by a long term agreement, or is it a purchase order relationship that the customer can terminate without consequence? They conduct independent interviews with key customers without the management team present, specifically to assess the strength and durability of the relationship and whether it is with the company or with the founder personally.

The price impact: Customer concentration above twenty percent in any single account, or above fifty percent in the top five accounts, produces a direct valuation discount that PE firms apply formulaically. A business with $5M in EBITDA and forty percent of its revenue in a single customer will be valued at a multiple one to two turns below a comparable business with a diversified customer base. On $5M of EBITDA, the difference between a five turn multiple and a four turn multiple is $5M of enterprise value. The concentration risk also typically produces a deal structure modification: an earnout tied to retention of the concentrated customer relationship, which transfers the concentration risk from the buyer to the seller in the post close period.

The pre process remedy: The concentration problem is addressed through deliberate new account development over a multi year period before any transaction process begins. The goal is to reduce the largest single customer to below twenty percent of revenue and the top five to below forty percent. This is not a presentation strategy, it is a business strategy that takes two to three years to execute and that makes the business genuinely less risky, not just less risky appearing. The customer interviews in diligence are addressed by transitioning key customer relationships from personal founder management to institutional account management: a formal account team, a documented relationship history in CRM, a service delivery record that exists independent of the founder's personal involvement.

Finding 3, Management Team Depth and Founder Dependency

What PE finds in diligence: The PE firm's operating partners conduct a direct assessment of every member of the senior leadership team, typically through structured interviews, reference calls that go beyond the management's suggested list, and operational observation of how decisions are made in the business. The specific question they are answering is not whether the management team performs well under current conditions. It is whether the management team will perform adequately after the founder's role changes, which it will in any transaction. They map the specific functions that are founder dependent, the key customer relationships that are personal rather than institutional, and the operational knowledge that lives in the founder's head rather than in documented systems.

The price impact: Significant founder dependency produces two transaction consequences. The first is a direct purchase price reduction reflecting the key man risk premium: the buyer is paying for an asset whose performance depends materially on a specific individual, and they discount that asset accordingly. The second is a structural consequence: an employment agreement that requires the founder to remain in an active operational role for two to four years post close, often with a portion of the purchase price held back in an earnout tied to the business's performance during the retention period. Founders who expected to step back significantly after closing discover that the transaction they worked toward requires continued active management of the business they sold.

The pre process remedy: Build genuine management depth in the two critical functions most likely to be assessed as founder dependent: sales and operations. Recruit outside talent with demonstrated experience at a comparable scale, integrate them with twelve months of structured support, and transfer genuine decision making authority. Document the operational practices, decision frameworks, and customer management protocols that currently exist only in the founder's tacit knowledge. Build a succession plan for each senior role. The management team that the diligence team assesses should be the team that could run the business without the founder in the building, because that is the team the buyer is underwriting.

Finding 4, Operational and Financial Infrastructure Gaps

What PE finds in diligence: The operational diligence team examines the systems, processes, and reporting infrastructure that supports the business's performance management. In mid-sized companies that have been built organically around a founder's management style, this infrastructure is frequently informal, founder dependent, and insufficient for the reporting requirements that PE ownership imposes from day one of the post close period. Specifically: the monthly close takes twenty or more days, producing financial statements that are too old to support active portfolio management. The management reporting package does not track the operational KPIs that the PE firm will use to assess business performance monthly.

The CRM system contains incomplete or inconsistent customer data. The financial systems cannot produce the segmented reporting, by customer, product, geography, that PE portfolio management requires.

The price impact: Operational infrastructure gaps produce a specific and underappreciated transaction cost: the cost of building the infrastructure post close rather than pre close is borne by the company rather than by the prior owner. A PE firm that acquires a business with a twenty five day close cycle, inadequate management reporting, and legacy financial systems will spend twelve to eighteen months and several hundred thousand dollars upgrading the infrastructure. That cost is incorporated into the value creation plan and correspondingly subtracted from the price they are willing to pay for the business as acquired. The owner who sells a business with a ten day close, a comprehensive management dashboard, and current financial systems is not just presenting a better business, he is transferring infrastructure the buyer would otherwise have had to build.

The pre process remedy: Implement the ten day monthly close eighteen to twenty four months before any contemplated transaction. Commission reviewed financial statements covering the prior three fiscal years. Build a weekly management reporting dashboard that tracks the five to seven operational metrics most directly predictive of financial performance. Implement a CRM system and populate it with complete, current customer data. Document the key operational processes in a format that a new owner's management team could use to understand how the business operates without direct knowledge transfer from the founder. This infrastructure is not built for the transaction, it makes the business better to manage in the present and more valuable at exit.

Finding 5, Legal, Compliance, and Contractual Exposures

What PE finds in diligence: The legal diligence team reviews every material contract, every pending or threatened litigation, every regulatory compliance obligation, and every intellectual property arrangement that affects the business. In mid-sized companies that have been operated informally, the legal review frequently uncovers: customer contracts that were never properly executed or that have lapsed without renewal; key employee agreements that do not contain enforceable non compete or intellectual property assignment provisions; supplier agreements that have auto renewed on terms that are no longer commercially favorable; intellectual property that was developed by contractors without proper assignment to the company; and compliance obligations, environmental, employment, data privacy, that have been managed informally rather than systematically.

The price impact: Legal exposures produce two distinct transaction consequences. The first is a specific price reduction or escrow holdback reflecting the quantified risk of the identified exposures. A pending employment claim, an unresolved customer contract dispute, or an environmental remediation obligation will be valued by the buyer's legal team and subtracted from the purchase price or held in escrow pending resolution. The second is a deal timeline extension that benefits the buyer. Every open legal item requires resolution before closing, or a specific indemnification structure that transfers the risk from the buyer to the seller. Both outcomes reduce the effective value of the transaction from the seller's perspective.

The pre process remedy: Engage a mid market M&A attorney to conduct a pre transaction legal audit covering all five exposure categories twelve to eighteen months before any process begins. Execute or renew all material customer contracts with properly drafted terms. Ensure all key employees have current agreements with enforceable non compete, non solicitation, and IP assignment provisions. Review and renegotiate supplier agreements that are no longer commercially favorable. Document the compliance management processes for all applicable regulatory obligations. The cost of this legal housekeeping is a small fraction of the price adjustment that unresolved legal exposures produce in a transaction.

What the Investment Banker's Presentation Cannot Fix

I want to address something directly, because it reflects a misunderstanding I have observed consistently on the sell side of transactions: the belief that a well constructed investment banker's presentation can manage around the problems that the business has not fixed.

The investment banker's presentation is an advocacy document. It is designed to present the business in its most favorable light, to frame the competitive position compellingly, to present the growth opportunity persuasively, and to tell the financial story in a way that supports the valuation the seller is seeking. Investment bankers are skilled at this work, and the best of them produce presentations that genuinely advance the transaction at the price the seller desires.

But the investment banker's presentation does not survive the diligence process intact. Every claim in it is tested. Every forward projection is stress tested against historical data. Every competitive advantage is examined for durability. Every customer relationship is evaluated for concentration and contractual protection. The presentation describes the business as the seller sees it. The diligence process reconstructs the business as it actually is.

I have reviewed hundreds of investment banker presentations from the buyer's side of the table. The presentations that were most effective were not the ones with the most compelling narrative or the most aggressive valuation argument. They were the ones that described a business whose diligence review confirmed rather than revised the presentation's claims. Those presentations were effective not because the banker was more skilled but because the underlying business had no significant gap between the presented picture and the actual one.

Conversely, the presentations that generated the most significant price adjustments in the diligence process were not necessarily the weakest presentations. Some of them were genuinely excellent narratives built on top of businesses that had not fixed their underlying problems. The excellence of the narrative made the price adjustment in diligence more painful, not less, because it set an expectation that the business subsequently failed to support.

The specific phrase I have used most often when reviewing businesses from the buying side is: the presentation is good but the business has not caught up with it yet. That phrase is the most precise description of what happens when a strong investment banker is engaged before the underlying problems have been addressed. The presentation describes a version of the company that could exist. The diligence process describes the version that does exist. The gap between them is the price adjustment.

The presentation gets you into the process. The price is earned years earlier, in operations that survive diligence.

The Deal Structure Consequences of Deferred Problems

Most discussions of transaction preparation focus on the purchase price. The purchase price is important. But in my experience as a sponsor and transaction participant, the deal structure is frequently more consequential to the seller's actual economic outcome than the headline purchase price. And it is the deal structure, the earnouts, the escrow holdbacks, the seller notes, the employment agreement requirements, that is most directly determined by the problems that the diligence process finds.

The Earnout: The Buyer's Risk Transfer Instrument

An earnout is a structure in which a portion of the purchase price is contingent on the business's performance after the transaction closes. From the buyer's perspective, it is a risk transfer mechanism: if the specific risks identified in diligence, customer concentration, management dependency, forward revenue assumptions, materialize negatively after closing, the earnout payment is reduced or eliminated, and the economic consequence falls on the seller rather than the buyer.

Earnouts appear in transactions where the buyer and seller cannot agree on the probability that the business's forward performance will justify the purchase price. They are almost always the consequence of an unresolved diligence risk that the buyer is unwilling to accept at full price and the seller is unwilling to discount at closing. The seller who walks into a process with unresolved customer concentration, unverified management depth, or forward revenue assumptions that the historical trend does not support is the seller who receives an earnout offer. The earnout might be structured to pay the full amount if the business performs as represented. In practice, earnouts are disputed at a rate that should terrify every seller who accepts one without fully understanding the enforcement risk.

The Escrow Holdback: The Indemnification Reserve

An escrow holdback is a portion of the purchase price, typically five to fifteen percent, that is held by a neutral escrow agent for an agreed period post close, subject to claims by the buyer for breaches of the seller's representations and warranties in the purchase agreement. The size and duration of the escrow are directly correlated with the number and severity of the legal and operational exposures found in diligence.

A clean business with no material legal exposures, fully documented contracts, and comprehensive compliance management will negotiate a modest escrow, typically five percent for twelve months. A business with unresolved contract disputes, incomplete employment agreements, or undocumented compliance practices will face a larger escrow, frequently ten to fifteen percent for twenty four months. On a $50M transaction, the difference between a $2.5M escrow and a $7.5M escrow is $5M of purchase price that the seller cannot access for twelve to twenty four months after closing.

The Employment Agreement: The Founder's Surprise

The employment agreement requirement is the transaction consequence that surprises founders most frequently and most painfully, because it contradicts the mental model of the transaction as a financial event that concludes at closing.

When a PE firm's diligence process identifies significant founder dependency, when the assessment reveals that key customer relationships, operational knowledge, or management credibility are concentrated in the founder's personal involvement, they address this risk through the deal structure. They require the founder to remain in an active management role for a defined post close period, typically two to four years, as a condition of the transaction. They attach a portion of the purchase price to the employment period through a combination of retention bonuses, deferred payments, and performance linked earnouts.

The founder who intended to transition out of day to day management within twelve months of closing discovers that the business he built around his personal involvement has made him a required asset in his own transaction. He is not selling and departing. He is selling and being retained, on terms that the buyer determined based on the dependency they found in diligence.

Diligence Finding	Typical Deal Structure Consequence
EBITDA quality gap above 20%	Price reduction equal to multiple applied to normalized EBITDA; potential deferred payment structure tied to earnings confirmation
Single customer above 25% of revenue	Earnout tied to customer retention; 1 2 multiple point discount on base valuation
Founder dependency in 2+ functions	Employment agreement requirement of 2 4 years; portion of purchase price tied to retention and performance
Management close cycle above 20 days	Infrastructure investment budget deducted from purchase price; operational improvement plan required pre close
Open legal exposures above $500K	Escrow holdback of 10 15% for 18 24 months; specific indemnification for identified exposures
Revenue recognition inconsistency	Normalized revenue basis for valuation; trailing revenue scrutiny extends diligence timeline 30 60 days

The Preparation Framework: Running Your Own Diligence Before They Do

The most powerful perspective shift available to a founder or CEO approaching a liquidity event is this: before a buyer runs diligence on your business, run it on yourself.

This is not a metaphor. It is a specific instruction. Engage the same categories of expertise that a PE buyer's diligence team will engage, a quality of earnings firm, a legal advisor with M&A experience, and an operational advisor with specific knowledge of the diligence standards applied in the relevant transaction market, and ask them to do to your business what the buyer's team will do. Find the gap between the business you believe you have and the business you actually have.

This exercise, conducted two to three years before the contemplated transaction, produces three outcomes that no amount of investment banker preparation can replicate.

First, it identifies the specific problems that the buyer's diligence team will find, in time for those problems to be addressed operationally rather than managed presentationally. A customer concentration problem identified three years before a transaction can be reduced through deliberate new account development. The same problem identified three months before cannot. An EBITDA normalization gap identified three years before a transaction can be eliminated by adjusting the financial management practices that created it. The same gap identified in diligence can only be negotiated, and it will be negotiated from a position of weakness.

Second, it produces the three year financial track record of the normalized business rather than the normalized at the last minute business. This distinction matters enormously in the quality of earnings analysis. A business that has been paying market rate compensation, eliminating personal expenses, and maintaining clean related party arrangements for three years presents a financial history that a buyer can evaluate with confidence. A business that made these changes in the six months before the process started presents changes that a buyer will scrutinize with skepticism and potentially discount as presentation rather than substance.

Third, it gives the seller the information advantage in the transaction. The seller who has already conducted quality of earnings analysis, legal housekeeping, and operational infrastructure assessment is not surprised in diligence. he is confirming, not discovering. The buyer's diligence team's findings become a validation of what he already knows rather than a series of revelations that shift the negotiating dynamic in the buyer's favor.

The cost of running your own diligence is modest relative to the transaction value at risk. A quality of earnings engagement covering three years of financial statements costs between thirty and eighty thousand dollars. A legal audit covering the five exposure categories described above costs between twenty and sixty thousand dollars. An operational assessment covering the infrastructure and management depth questions costs between twenty five and fifty thousand dollars. The total investment is between seventy five and two hundred thousand dollars. On a transaction where the diligence findings have historically reduced the seller's proceeds by five to twenty percent, that investment has a return that no other pre transaction activity can match.

Hire the quality of earnings firm before the buyer does. Otherwise you'll end the process negotiating against findings you can't dispute.

What I Learned From the Buying Side That I Now Apply From the Advising Side

Having spent years reviewing companies as a sponsor and private equity participant, and now spending years helping owners prepare companies for capital events, I want to share several specific observations that have shaped how I think about what distinguishes transactions that achieve their potential from those that do not.

The Business That Closes on Time at the Expected Price Is Not Lucky

In every transaction I participated in from the buying side, the deals that closed on time, at or near the initially indicated price, with minimal structural modifications, shared a specific characteristic: the business had been prepared. Not by the investment banker in the six months before the process started. By the owner in the two to three years before the investment banker was engaged. The financial statements were clean and had been clean for long enough to constitute a track record. The management team could speak to the business's performance and strategy with authority and depth that did not depend on the CEO being in the room. The customer relationships were documented and diversified. The legal house was in order.

These businesses did not have lower diligence findings. They had different diligence findings, findings that confirmed the investment banker's narrative rather than revising it. The quality of earnings analysis produced a normalized EBITDA that was close to the reported EBITDA. The customer interviews confirmed the relationship quality and durability that the management presentation described. The management assessment identified a team with genuine depth and real independent authority. The legal review found no material exposures. Each of these outcomes was not the result of a favorable draw. It was the result of deliberate preparation.

The Most Expensive Mistakes Are Made Before the Process Starts

As a buyer, I observed that the most significant value transfers from seller to buyer in mid-sized transactions did not occur in the negotiation of the purchase price. They occurred in the three to five years before the transaction, when the seller made or failed to make the specific operational and financial decisions that determined what diligence would find.

The owner who paid himself above market compensation for three years was not making a business decision. He was making a transaction decision, because every dollar of above market compensation was a dollar subtracted from the EBITDA that would determine his exit multiple. He just did not know he was making a transaction decision, because nobody had explained to him that every financial management decision he made during the operating years of the business was simultaneously a transaction preparation decision.

This is the perspective shift I work hardest to create in the founders and CEOs I advise: the recognition that every significant business decision made in the three years before a contemplated transaction is also a transaction preparation decision. The hiring decision, the customer relationship investment, the financial reporting improvement, the legal housekeeping, the management depth investment, each of these creates or eliminates a diligence finding that will appear in the transaction negotiation in direct proportion to the care or neglect with which it was managed.

Buyers Do Not Negotiate Against Problems They Did Not Expect to Find

One of the most consistent patterns I observed from the buying side was this: diligence findings that we expected to find, that the management presentation had flagged, that the data room had documented, that the seller had disclosed proactively, were priced into our initial indication of interest. They were not used as renegotiation ammunition in the final round. Diligence findings that we did not expect to find, that contradicted the management presentation, that the data room had not documented, that the seller had not disclosed, became the basis of late stage price adjustments and structural modifications.

The lesson from this observation is direct: disclose proactively and early. The seller who identifies her company's specific risks and discloses them clearly in the management presentation and the data room is the seller who controls the pricing of those risks. The buyer has already incorporated them into the initial indication. The seller who allows those risks to be discovered in diligence is the seller who experiences them as late stage surprises that shift the negotiating dynamic entirely in the buyer's favor.

The best deals don't go to the best businesses. They go to the most prepared sellers.

The Instruction That Summarizes Everything

I have been direct throughout this article about what private equity finds and what it costs. I want to close with equal directness about what the owner who wants a different outcome should do.

Start three years earlier than you think you need to. The problems that cost owners the most in transactions are not the ones that develop in the six months before the process starts. They are the ones that accumulated over years of operating the business in ways that made personal sense and transactional cost. You cannot fix three years of accumulated EBITDA normalization gaps in six months. You cannot build three years of clean financial track record in six months. You cannot reduce customer concentration from forty percent to twenty percent in six months. You cannot build genuine management depth in six months.

Find the problems yourself, before the buyer does. Engage a quality of earnings firm. Engage an M&A attorney. Engage an operational advisor with specific knowledge of what buyers in your transaction market look for. Run your own diligence process with the specific objective of identifying every finding that the buyer's team will find, and then fix the ones that can be fixed, document the ones that cannot, and price the ones that require disclosure into your expectations before the process begins.

Remember that the investment banker is your advocate in the transaction market, not your preparation resource. He will present your business compellingly. He will access the right buyers. He will run an efficient process. But he cannot fix the problems that diligence will find, and he cannot create the three year track record that the quality of earnings analysis will reconstruct. That work must be done before he is engaged, not while he is running the process.

I have watched too many owners spend fifteen or twenty years building something genuinely valuable and then leave a meaningful portion of that value on the table in a transaction that could have been better, not because the business was not good enough, but because the preparation was not thorough enough and did not start early enough.

The business you have built deserves a transaction outcome that reflects its genuine worth. Getting there is not primarily a function of finding the right buyer or the right banker or the right market conditions. It is primarily a function of starting the preparation early enough, being honest about what you find when you look, and fixing what can be fixed before the buyer's team is in the building.

That work is available to you. The only question is whether you begin it when it is most useful, or wait until it is too late to matter.

Summary

The value of this chapter is not in showing that private equity is rigorous. Most founders already sense that. Its value is in making clear that the issues diligence surfaces are rarely hidden mysteries. They are deferred problems. EBITDA quality, customer concentration, founder dependency, infrastructure weakness, and legal exposure are not exotic findings. They are ordinary consequences of how privately owned businesses evolve over time. The difference is timing. Found by the seller before the process begins, they become preparation projects. Found by the buyer during the process, they become price chips, escrow demands, earnouts, and leverage shifting late in the negotiation.

One of the structural reasons those findings become more expensive is the capital structure wrapped around them. The next chapter turns to that issue directly and examines how a capital structure that once made sense can become a steady discount on enterprise value later.

18

The Capital Structure That Made Sense at Twenty Million Is Destroying Value at Sixty Million

Today's funding can be tomorrow's ceiling.

There is a conversation I have had more times than I can count, and it follows the same arc almost every time.

A founder comes looking for capital to fund the next phase of a company that has grown into something real. Revenue is often between twenty million and sixty million. The business is credible. The growth story is genuine. The market opportunity is there. Then I ask about the capital structure, and the mood changes.

There is a private credit facility priced for a smaller and riskier company. There is a convertible note from an early believer whose terms no longer reflect what the company has become. There is sometimes a revenue sharing instrument that looked flexible at ten million in revenue and feels punitive at forty. There are personal guarantees that still tie the founder's balance sheet to business obligations long after the company should have graduated beyond them.

None of these decisions were irrational when they were made. They solved real problems at the time. The issue is that they were designed for an earlier version of the company. What once enabled growth now consumes cash, narrows strategic options, and suppresses value.

A capital structure is not a permanent fact about a business. It is a collection of financing decisions made under specific conditions. When the company outgrows those conditions, the structure does not update itself. Management has to update it deliberately, and preferably before the mismatch is actively destroying value.

Capital structure isn't a finance issue. It's strategy, expressed in financial terms.

How Capital Structure Mismatches Form

Most mid-sized company balance sheets are not the result of a coherent capital strategy. They are the result of a capital history. The founder raised what was available when the company needed it, on the terms that were offered, from the providers willing to engage at that stage of risk.

That is understandable. It is also how complexity accumulates. A company that now looks mature and financeable can still be carrying multiple layers of capital that were priced for a very different risk profile. The debt agreements come from different years, different lenders, and different assumptions. The equity instruments reflect old valuation caps and old negotiating leverage. The obligations fit together because they have been tolerated, not because they were designed to work together.

The result is often not financial distress. It is financial constraint. The company can operate, but it cannot move with the freedom its current scale should support. Capital that should be funding growth is instead servicing history.

The Four Mismatches That Cause the Most Damage

High Cost Private Debt With Restrictive Covenants

This is the most common mismatch I see. Early in the company's life, private credit was the only realistic option. The lender priced the risk accordingly, often with double digit interest, floating rates, and covenants tight enough to give the lender comfort when the business was smaller and less proven.

Years later, the company is larger, more diversified, and meaningfully less risky. Yet the debt still carries terms meant for the earlier business. The founder is paying premium pricing for capital the company could now access at much better terms. Worse, the covenant package often does more damage than the rate. Management starts filtering operating decisions through leverage tests, fixed charge coverage, and consent requirements that should no longer be central to running the business.

The real cost is not only the interest differential. It is the acquisition that could not be pursued, the hiring decision delayed, the capital expenditure pushed out, and the management time consumed by staying inside constraints that belong to an earlier chapter.

Convertible Notes and Early Investor Overhangs

Convertible notes are often perfectly sensible when a company is small and proving itself. They let the founder raise capital without trying to negotiate a full pricing event before the business has earned one.

The problem emerges later, when old valuation caps, discounts, and conversion rights remain outstanding as the company reaches a much larger scale.

At that point the issue is not simply dilution. It is complexity. New investors want to know exactly what the company looks like on a fully diluted basis, how outstanding notes convert under different scenarios, and whether legacy instruments distort the economics of a new financing round. When the answer is messy, the company loses speed, leverage, and sometimes interested investors altogether.

A growth capital provider can accept complexity when the underlying business quality is extraordinary. But no one pays extra for complexity. They price it as friction, governance risk, and uncertainty.

Revenue Based Financing That Outlived Its Usefulness

Revenue based structures are attractive for an obvious reason. They appear flexible, they avoid immediate dilution, and they often arrive faster than institutional debt. At a small scale, the repayment percentage can feel manageable.

As the company grows, the same repayment formula can become punishing. A percentage of revenue that looked modest at ten million can consume a meaningful amount of free cash flow at forty million, especially when the company is trying to reinvest aggressively in growth. The true annualized cost of this capital is often far higher than founders appreciate because providers rarely frame it in the language of comparable borrowing costs.

The strategic cost is larger than the financing cost alone. The company is sacrificing future growth investment to pay for yesterday's growth capital on terms that no longer fit the business.

Personal Guarantees and Founder Balance Sheet Entanglement

Personal guarantees are often the price of getting the first real debt facility done. At the beginning, that may be the only path. The problem is when the company has grown enough to support institutional lending on its own merits and the founder is still carrying personal exposure that should have been removed years earlier.

A founder whose personal balance sheet is tied to the company's obligations behaves differently, often more cautiously, than one whose exposure is limited to equity. That caution may be understandable, but it becomes strategically expensive when the business reaches a stage where bold but rational investment decisions carry the highest returns.

The guarantee is not just a legal provision. It is a management constraint. It changes the founder's posture toward risk, and in growth businesses that posture matters.

What Growth Capital Providers Actually See

When a company with a mismatched structure comes looking for new capital, we do not begin with the financing problem. We begin with the quality of the business. If the business is attractive, the capital structure can often be fixed. But the condition of the capital structure still changes what terms are possible and how quickly we can get there.

A clean structure lets the conversation focus on deploying fresh capital into growth. A messy one forces the first hour into untangling history. How much of the new money goes to refinance old debt. What happens when the notes convert. Which rights survive. Which lenders must consent. Which guarantees remain. Every layer of complexity consumes time, fees, and negotiating energy.

It also sends a signal about financial management sophistication. That signal is not always fair, but it is real. A founder who has allowed an obviously outdated structure to persist may be seen as someone who has not yet built the financial architecture a larger company requires. That perception affects terms even when the business itself is strong.

The growth capital conversation you want is about how to accelerate a good business. The conversation you do not want is about why the existing capital structure has to be repaired before growth can even be discussed.

Designing the Capital Structure for the Next Three Years

The right question is not what capital can we raise right now. The right question is what capital structure does this business need for the next three years of growth, and what sequence gets us there with the least friction and the highest flexibility.

That mindset changes the process from capital procurement to capital design. Instead of taking whatever is available at the moment of need, management defines the target architecture first and then uses financing choices to move deliberately toward it.

In most mid-sized companies, that target structure has four layers. First, senior secured bank debt as the foundation when the company has the EBITDA and reporting quality to support it. Second, subordinated debt only when a defined initiative justifies the cost and the leverage can come down quickly. Third, minority growth equity when the company needs capital and strategic support without the burden of debt service. Fourth, strategic partnership capital only when the commercial value of the partner is real enough to justify the governance and ownership implications.

Senior Secured Bank Debt

Best for companies with at least eighteen to twenty four months of stable EBITDA, current reporting, and real collateral support. This should usually be the first layer evaluated because it is the least expensive and most efficient capital available to a qualified business.

Subordinated Debt

Useful when senior debt is already optimized and a specific initiative justifies additional leverage. It should be used selectively and modeled on a fully loaded cost basis, including warrants or other equity features.

Growth Equity

Appropriate when the company needs meaningful capital and strategic flexibility, and the founder is willing to exchange some dilution for balance sheet strength, governance support, and no fixed debt service burden.

Strategic Partner Capital

Best when the partner brings more than money, such as distribution, market access, technology, or customers. It should not be used simply because the capital is available.

The Refinancing Sequence That Usually Works Best

In most cases, order matters. The best first step is to address the most expensive debt. Doing that creates immediate cash flow relief and often funds the work required for the next steps.

Next, simplify cap table overhang from old notes or legacy investor structures. Until the fully diluted economics are clean and legible, new investors will discount the opportunity or avoid it entirely.

Then remove revenue sharing or royalty style obligations that drain free cash flow. After that, push to release personal guarantees once the company's actual credit quality supports it. Finally, approach growth equity or other strategic capital from a structure that is already comprehensible, financeable, and aligned with the business as it exists today.

What a Deliberate Capital Strategy Produces

First, it lowers the cost of capital in a way that compounds. A seven point reduction in borrowing cost on a meaningful debt balance is not merely a finance improvement. It is growth capital that no longer leaks out through interest expense.

Second, it restores strategic flexibility. A company with the right debt terms can make acquisitions, invest in systems, and hire ahead of growth without treating every decision as a covenant event.

Third, it improves access to future capital. Clean structures raise faster and on better terms because new providers are evaluating business quality rather than untangling legacy financing.

Finally, it improves enterprise value. A company whose reported economics reflect its real operating economics, without the drag of outdated financing arrangements, is simply worth more.

The Conversation Every Founder Should Have Before Capital Is Needed

Every founder of a mid-sized company should conduct a complete capital structure review at least every eighteen to twenty four months. Not when a raise is already underway. Not when a covenant issue has become urgent. Before the urgency.

The review should answer five questions. What is the all in cost of each element of the current structure. What would that same capital cost if originated today given the company's current scale and performance. What strategic actions is the structure preventing or delaying. When can each major element be refinanced or retired without excessive penalty. And what does the target structure need to look like three years from now.

These questions convert capital from a reactive necessity into a management discipline. They also force the founder to see that every financing choice is simultaneously a strategic choice, because every financing term changes what the business is free to do next.

The capital structure that made sense at twenty million is not the right structure for a sixty million dollar company. The work of getting from one to the other is not glamorous, but it is among the highest return uses of management attention available to a growing company.

Every dollar of above market financing cost removed is a dollar available for growth. Every covenant simplified is a strategic option unlocked. Every personal guarantee released is management judgment freed from unnecessary fear.

Summary

Every financing decision examined in this chapter was rational when it was made. The private credit facility funded growth when bank debt was unavailable. The convertible note solved a capital problem at a time when the business had few options. Revenue based financing preserved ownership when dilution felt unacceptable. Personal guarantees got deals closed that otherwise would not have closed.

The problem is not that these choices were wrong. The problem is that they were made for an earlier version of the company. Once the business has grown, those same structures quietly begin to suppress flexibility, absorb cash, complicate future capital raises, and reduce the multiple a sophisticated buyer is willing to pay. A clean structure amplifies every other preparation effort. A mismatched one discounts them.

19

Why the Last Two Years Determine the Multiple

YOUR LIQUIDITY EVENT IS BUILT ON YOUR LAST TWO YEARS — NOT YOUR STORY.

I want to explain the financial mechanism behind the trailing period asymmetry, because understanding it specifically changes how a founder thinks about the two years before a transaction in a way that generic advice about 'exit preparation' does not.

A sophisticated buyer, private equity, strategic acquiror, growth capital investor, values a mid-sized company based on two variables: the normalized EBITDA they will use as the earnings base, and the multiple they will apply to it. Both variables are primarily determined by the company's trailing performance, and both are more sensitive to recent performance than to historical performance.

The earnings base is typically calculated as a weighted average of the last two to three years of normalized EBITDA, with the most recent year receiving the highest weight. In most transaction models I have been involved in, the trailing twelve months receives twice the weight of the year two years prior. A company whose EBITDA has improved from three million dollars to four million dollars to five million dollars over three years is valued significantly higher than one whose EBITDA has been flat at four million for three years, even though the average of the three year series is nearly identical. The direction of travel over the recent period is the signal the buyer is buying.

The multiple is not a fixed number that the buyer applies mechanically. It is a judgment that reflects their confidence in the sustainability and trajectory of the earnings base. A company with a clear upward EBITDA trend, improving margins, growing net revenue retention, and a management team that has been building capability over the prior two years commands a premium multiple over the same company with flat metrics. The premium is not marginal. In a mid-sized transaction, the difference between a five times multiple and a six times multiple on four million dollars of EBITDA is four million dollars of enterprise value, the entire value of a year's earnings.

The combined effect of improved earnings base and premium multiple in a company that has actively performed in the two years before a transaction is multiplicative, not additive. On a base of five million dollars of EBITDA, the difference between a flat performance trajectory and a twenty percent improvement trajectory, combined with the multiple premium that trajectory commands, is typically ten to fifteen million dollars of additional enterprise value. That is the financial argument for treating the two years before the event as the highest leverage period in the company's history.

The multiple isn't a reward for the past. It's a bet on the future — and your last two years are the only evidence.

The Mindset Shift: From Running the Business to Building the Asset

The most important change that must occur in the two years before a capital event is not operational or financial. It is cognitive. It is a specific shift in how the founder or CEO thinks about what they are doing every day.

For most of the company's life, the founder has been running a business. The goal has been to make the business work: to find customers, to serve them well, to manage the costs, to grow the revenue, to deal with the problems that arise. This mindset is entirely appropriate for the operating phase of a company's development. It is what produced the company's success.

In the two years before a capital event, a second mindset must operate simultaneously alongside the operating mindset. The second mindset is that of a builder building an asset, a specific, transferable, documented, demonstrably performing asset that a sophisticated outside party will evaluate, underwrite, and purchase. The builder of assets mindset asks different questions than the operator mindset. Not 'what do I need to do today to keep the business running?' but 'what does this business need to look like in twenty four months so that a sophisticated buyer will see what I know it to be?'

These mindsets are not incompatible. The business must still be run while the asset is being built. But they require different disciplines, different time allocations, and different decision filters. The operator optimizes for today. The asset builder optimizes for the picture a buyer will see in twenty four months. Every significant management decision in the two year window should be evaluated against both filters: does this make the business run better today, and does it make the asset more demonstrably valuable in twenty four months?

When the two filters point in different directions, when the operationally convenient decision is the one that makes the asset less legible to a buyer, or when the asset building decision requires a short term operational sacrifice, the founder in the two year window must be willing to apply the asset building filter with more weight than he has historically applied to any consideration other than making the business work.

OPERATING MINDSET	TRANSACTION MINDSET
Hire a junior accountant because the business needs financial support and the cost is manageable	Upgrade to a controller with QoE experience because the financial reporting quality will be scrutinized in diligence and the cost is minimal compared to the value it protects
Continue the above market owner compensation because the business can afford it and it is personal financial optimization	Normalize owner compensation to market rate now so that three years of clean EBITDA exist before the quality of earnings analysis asks why the number changed
Manage the largest customer relationship personally because it is the most efficient way to maintain the relationship	Transition the relationship to an institutional account team now so that a buyer can see the relationship survives independent of the founder's personal involvement
Accept the revenue based financing renewal because the business needs working capital and the terms are familiar	Refinance to senior bank debt now so that the cost of capital is normalized and the management reporting reflects the true operating economics rather than above market financing costs

The Two Years Before the Exit Are Worth More Than the Twenty Before Them

The enterprise value a sophisticated buyer assigns to your business is shaped primarily by the last twenty four months of performance, not the prior two decades. Most founders discover that too late to do anything about it.

The conversation I have had most often with founders in the months following a capital event is not the celebratory one people expect. It is a quieter conversation, usually over coffee some weeks after the closing, when the transaction is complete and the founder has had time to reflect on what the process actually produced versus what he had expected it to produce.

The reflection is almost always the same. The business was good. The investment banker was competent. The buyer was credible. But the final number was lower than expected, or the deal structure was more complicated than expected, or the earnout that was supposed to be achievable turned out to reflect a risk the buyer had identified that the founder had not fully appreciated. And when I ask what happened in the twelve months before the process started, the answer is almost always some version of: I was running the business. I was doing what I always do.

That is the problem. In the twelve to twenty four months before a liquidity event, doing what you always do is the single most expensive strategic error available to a mid-sized company owner or CEO. Because what a sophisticated buyer uses to value the business is not the twenty years of accumulated history you have built. It is the trajectory of the last two years, the direction the business is moving, the pace at which it is improving, the quality of the financial performance in the most recent reporting periods, and the evidence that the management team can sustain and extend that performance after the founder's role changes.

The asymmetry is stark and it is real. A company that has generated consistent fifteen percent EBITDA margins for a decade but has improved to eighteen percent in the last two years commands a materially higher multiple than the same company that peaked at eighteen percent four years ago and has settled back to fifteen. The trajectory matters more than the average. The recency matters more than the history. The trend the buyer is buying is the one visible in the trailing twenty four months, and that trend, upward, flat, or downward, is the primary determinant of the multiple applied to the earnings.

This chapter is a direct instruction to every founder and owner CEO who is contemplating a capital event in the next two to four years. Not a planning framework, not a strategic review process, not a transaction preparation checklist. A direct instruction: the two years before the event are your highest leverage professional opportunity, and they require a specific change in mindset, a specific change in focus, and a level of concentrated managerial intensity that the normal operating mode of running a business does not produce.

The founder who runs the business as usual in the two years before a capital event is not making a neutral choice. He is making the most expensive choice available to him, leaving the value of a lifetime of work on the table because he did not understand that the last chapter of the company's story determines how the whole story is valued.

AFTERWORD

The Argument the Book Makes

Nineteen chapters across five domains produce a single coherent argument, and it is worth stating it plainly.

Every gap described in this book — the gap between complexity and growth, between financial statements and operational reality, between strategic intent and organizational behavior, between reported earnings and normalized earnings, between the management team the founder believes he has and the one a buyer evaluates, between what the board sees and what is actually happening — is a gap between what the company appears to be and what it actually is.

These gaps are not the product of dishonesty. They are the product of the natural human tendency to see a company through the lens of one's investment in it — to see what was hoped for rather than what precisely exists. That tendency is not a failure. It is the same optimism and conviction that builds companies. It is, however, a tendency with a specific cost when it prevents the honest diagnostic assessment that every consequential management decision requires.

The discipline that runs through every chapter of this book is the discipline of honest diagnosis. Not the comfortable diagnosis. Not the politically acceptable one. The honest one — the kind an engineer brings to a system failure, a physician brings to a clinical presentation, a sophisticated investor brings to a due diligence process. The companies that reach their potential are the ones whose leadership applied that discipline to the decisions described in these pages, at the moments when those decisions were available to be made. The ones that fell short are the ones that deferred the diagnosis until it arrived as a consequence rather than a choice.

Every gap is findable. Most are fixable. The ones found too late become the most expensive tuition in business.

That tuition is avoidable. It has been for every company this book was written from. The purpose of writing it down is to make it avoidable for the companies it was written for.

About the Author

Joseph P. Lahey has spent his career at the intersection of operating leadership, capital markets, and ownership transition in mid-sized companies — occupying every significant role available in that world and drawing from each one the specific perspective that this book reflects.

He began his career as an engineer, a background whose diagnostic orientation has informed every management role he has held since. As an executive, he served as CEO and Chairman of two public companies that each exceeded one hundred million dollars in revenue, and as owner-CEO of private operating businesses across multiple sectors including industrial services, fabrication, and technology-enabled services. He has managed companies through growth phases, through restructuring, and through the specific operational and financial challenges that the growth stage imposes on mid-sized company leadership.

As a capital market participant, he has been a sponsor and private equity participant in transactions spanning the full range of mid-sized company capital events — recapitalizations, strategic sales, growth equity raises, and management buyouts. He has reviewed hundreds of companies from the buyer's side of the table and has structured and negotiated transactions from both the investing and operating sides. That dual perspective, accumulated across a career of active participation rather than observation, is the foundation of the chapters in this book that address what sophisticated capital providers find in mid-sized companies and what it costs owners who let them find it first.

He now works as a principal investor and operating advisor, working alongside founders and management teams as they navigate the specific decisions that determine whether a mid-sized company reaches its potential or falls short of it. His advisory work spans the full arc of the company's development — from the operational disciplines of the early growth stage to the transaction preparation work of the years before a capital event — and is grounded in the conviction that the most valuable guidance available to a mid-sized company executive is the kind that comes from someone who has been in the same room, at the same table, facing the same decisions.

He is available for speaking engagements, executive advisory engagements, and principal investment discussions. He can be reached at jlahey@laheygrowthcapital.com.

www.ingramcontent.com/pod-product-compliance
Lightning Source LLC
LaVergne TN
LVHW052036200926
848481LV00005B/1702
9798996897506